C BUILDER AND WBEMSCRIPTING

Working with ExecQuery and
__InstanceDeletionEvent

Richard Thomas Edwards

Getting Started

THIS IS A BOOK OF CODE. It includes ASP, ASPX, HTA and HTML Reports and tables being generated by WbemScripting and ExecNotificationQuery to power them.

No book is perfect and I'm sure you will find the usual small coding issues a book of this size is naturally going to have.

Aside from that, both table and report type views are part of the source code and each of those use an assortment of controls. Below, is 99% of the pure code this book will be using. I say 99% because when the Excel Code is displayed, it uses the horizontal code for horizontal and vertical spreadsheet rendering. Also, the top up to where the enumerators start and the GetValue function will not be used in any of the coding examples. The size of this book would easily double. Instead, they are listed here and in the appendixes.

```
//----------------------------------------------------------------
#include <vcl.h>
#pragma hdrstop
#include "ComObj.hpp"
#include "Unit1.h"
#include <iostream>
#include <utility>
using namespace std;
//----------------------------------------------------------------
----------
#pragma package(smart_init)
#pragma resource "*.dfm"
TForm1 *Form1;
//----------------------------------------------------------------
----------
___fastcall TForm1::TForm1(TComponent* Owner)
```

```
          : TForm(Owner)
{
}
//-----------------------------------------------------------------

String* Names;
String** Values;

int v = 0;
int w = 0;

void WriteTheCode()
{

   Variant ws = Variant::CreateObject("WScript.Shell");
   String CurrentDirectory = ws.OlePropertyGet("CurrentDirectory");
   CurrentDirectory = CurrentDirectory + "\\Win32_Process.asp";
   Variant fso = Variant::CreateObject("Scripting.FileSystemObject");
   Variant txtstream = fso.OleFunction("OpenTextFile",
OleVariant(CurrentDirectory), OleVariant(2), OleVariant(true), OleVariant(-2));
   txtstream.OleFunction("WriteLine",OleVariant("<html
xmlns='http://www.w3.org/1999/xhtml'>"));
   txtstream.OleFunction("WriteLine",OleVariant("<head>"));
   txtstream.OleFunction("WriteLine",OleVariant("<title>Win32_Process</title>"));
   txtstream.OleFunction("WriteLine",OleVariant("</head>"));
   txtstream.OleFunction("WriteLine",OleVariant("<body>"));
   txtstream.OleFunction("WriteLine",OleVariant("<table border='0' Cellspacing='3'
cellpadding = '3'>"));
   txtstream.OleFunction("WriteLine",OleVariant("<%"));
   txtstream.OleFunction("WriteLine",OleVariant("Response.Write(\"<tr>\" +
vbcrlf))"));
   for(int b = 0; b < w; b++)
   {
      txtstream.OleFunction("WriteLine",OleVariant("Response.Write(\"<th
style='font-family:Calibri, Sans-Serif;font-size: 12px;color:darkred;' align='left'
nowrap='nowrap'>" + Names[b] + "</th>\" + vbcrlf))"));
   }
   txtstream.OleFunction("WriteLine",OleVariant("Response.Write(\"</tr>\" +
vbcrlf))"));
   for(int a = 0; a < v; a++)
   {
      txtstream.OleFunction("WriteLine",OleVariant("Response.Write(\"<tr>\" +
vbcrlf))"));
      for(int b = 0; b < w; b++)
      {
         txtstream.OleFunction("WriteLine",OleVariant("Response.Write(\"<td
style='font-family:Calibri, Sans-Serif;font-size: 12px;color:navy;' align='left'
nowrap='nowrap'>" + Values[a][b] + "</td>\" + vbcrlf))"));
      }
```

```
    txtstream.OleFunction("WriteLine",OleVariant("Response.Write(\"</tr>\" +
vbcrlf))"));
  }
  txtstream.OleFunction("WriteLine",OleVariant("%>"));
  txtstream.OleFunction("WriteLine",OleVariant("</table>"));
  txtstream.OleFunction("WriteLine",OleVariant("</body>"));
  txtstream.OleFunction("WriteLine",OleVariant("</html>"));
  txtstream.OleFunction("Close");
}
String GetValue(String N, Variant obj)
{
  int pos = 0;
  String Tempstr = obj.OleFunction("GetObjectText_");
  N = N + " = ";
  String Ne = N;
  pos = AnsiPos(Ne, Tempstr);
  if(pos > 0)
  {
    pos = pos + Ne.Length();
    int l = Tempstr.Length();
    Tempstr = Tempstr.SubString(pos, l);
    pos = AnsiPos(";", Tempstr);
    Tempstr = Tempstr.SubString(2, pos -3);
    return Tempstr;
  }
  else
  {
    return "";
  }
}
void BuildTheArray(Variant es)
{
        LPUNKNOWN punkEnum;
        IEnumVARIANT * propEnum=NULL;
        VARIANT tprop;
        VariantInit(&tprop);
        int nIndex;
        unsigned long c;

        while(v < 4)
        {

                Variant o = es.OleFunction("NextEvent", OleVariant(-1));
                Variant props = o.OlePropertyGet("Properties_");
                Variant Item = props.OleFunction("Item",
OleVariant("TargetInstance"));
                Variant obj = Item.OlePropertyGet("Value");
                Variant propSet = obj.OlePropertyGet("Properties_");
                w = propSet.OlePropertyGet("Count");
                        if(v == 0)
```

```
                {
                        int x = 0;
                        Names = new String[w];
                        Values = new String*[4];
                        for(int i = 0; i < 4; i++)
                        {
                                Values[i] = new String[w];
                        }
                        punkEnum = propSet.OlePropertyGet("_NewEnum");
                        punkEnum->QueryInterface(IID_IEnumVARIANT,
(LPVOID far*)&propEnum);
                        propEnum->AddRef();
                        punkEnum->Release();
                        while(propEnum->Next(1, &tprop, &c) == S_OK)
                        {
                                Variant prop = Variant(tprop);
                                String Name = prop.OlePropertyGet("Name");
                                Names[x] = Name;
                                String Value = GetValue(Name, obj);
                                Values[v][x] = Value;
                                x = x + 1;
                        }
                        x = 0;
                }
                else
                {
                        int x = 0;
                        punkEnum = propSet.OlePropertyGet("_NewEnum");
                        punkEnum->QueryInterface(IID_IEnumVARIANT,
(LPVOID far*)&propEnum);
                        propEnum->AddRef();
                        punkEnum->Release();

                        while(propEnum->Next(1, &tprop, &c) == S_OK)
                        {
                                Variant prop = Variant(tprop);
                                String Name = prop.OlePropertyGet("Name");
                                String Value = GetValue(Name, obj);
                                Values[v][x] = Value;
                                x = x + 1;
                        }

                }
                v=v+1;
        }
        WriteTheCode();
 }
```

```
void __fastcall TForm1::FormCreate(TObject *Sender)
{

        Variant L = Variant::CreateObject("WbemScripting.SWbemLocator");
        Variant svc = L.OleFunction("ConnectServer", OleVariant("."),
OleVariant("root\\CIMV2"));
        Variant security = svc.OlePropertyGet("Security_");
        security.OlePropertySet("AuthenticationLevel", 6);
        security.OlePropertySet("ImpersonationLevel", 3);
        String strQuery = "Select * From __InstanceDeletionEvent WITHIN 1 where
targetInstance ISA'Win32_Process'";
        Variant es = svc.OleFunction("ExecNotificationQuery",
OleVariant(strQuery));

        BuildTheArray(es);

}
```

Okay, so what is all that code above doing, right? Well, to begin with it starts off creating a WbemScripting.SWbemLocator object that we use to connect to WMI with and then walks through a couple of DCOM security settings and then uses Get to give us an object that then gives us the instances or collection of objects we can then use to create the arrays needed to populate the names and the values.

After that, the information is digested by the code that was selected from below and the output is written to a file that completes the process. The code that we're going to be deleting and rebuilding is inside the WriteTheCode sub routine:

```
void WriteTheCode()
{
  Variant ws = Variant::CreateObject("WScript.Shell");
  String CurrentDirectory = ws.OlePropertyGet("CurrentDirectory");
  CurrentDirectory = CurrentDirectory + "\\Win32_Process.asp";
  Variant fso = Variant::CreateObject("Scripting.FileSystemObject");
  Variant txtstream = fso.OleFunction("OpenTextFile",
OleVariant(CurrentDirectory), OleVariant(2), OleVariant(true), OleVariant(-2));
  txtstream.OleFunction("WriteLine",OleVariant("<html
xmlns='http://www.w3.org/1999/xhtml'>"));
  txtstream.OleFunction("WriteLine",OleVariant("<head>"));
  txtstream.OleFunction("WriteLine",OleVariant("<title>Win32_Process</title>"));
  txtstream.OleFunction("WriteLine",OleVariant("</head>"));
  txtstream.OleFunction("WriteLine",OleVariant("<body>"));
  txtstream.OleFunction("WriteLine",OleVariant("<table border='0' Cellspacing='3'
cellpadding = '3'>"));
  txtstream.OleFunction("WriteLine",OleVariant("<%"));
```

```
    txtstream.OleFunction("WriteLine",OleVariant("Response.Write(\"<tr>\" +
vbcrlf))"));
    for(int b = 0; b < w; b++)
    {
        txtstream.OleFunction("WriteLine",OleVariant("Response.Write(\"<th
style='font-family:Calibri, Sans-Serif;font-size: 12px;color:darkred;' align='left'
nowrap='nowrap'>" + Names[b] + "</th>\" + vbcrlf))"));
    }
    txtstream.OleFunction("WriteLine",OleVariant("Response.Write(\"</tr>\" +
vbcrlf))"));
    for(int a = 0; a < v; a++)
    {
        txtstream.OleFunction("WriteLine",OleVariant("Response.Write(\"<tr>\" +
vbcrlf))"));
        for(int b = 0; b < w; b++)
        {
            txtstream.OleFunction("WriteLine",OleVariant("Response.Write(\"<td
style='font-family:Calibri, Sans-Serif;font-size: 12px;color:navy;' align='left'
nowrap='nowrap'>" + Values[a][b] + "</td>\" + vbcrlf))"));
        }
        txtstream.OleFunction("WriteLine",OleVariant("Response.Write(\"</tr>\" +
vbcrlf))"));
    }
    txtstream.OleFunction("WriteLine",OleVariant("%>"));
    txtstream.OleFunction("WriteLine",OleVariant("</table>"));
    txtstream.OleFunction("WriteLine",OleVariant("</body>"));
    txtstream.OleFunction("WriteLine",OleVariant("</html>"));
    txtstream.OleFunction("Close");

}
```

So, the rest of the code is at the bottom of this book, allowing you to focus on the routine you want to use. Cutting and pasting all of it together so you can build whatever you want when it is needed.

Let's get started, shall we?

ASP Reports

Begin Code

```
Variant ws = Variant::CreateObject("WScript.Shell");
String CurrentDirectory = ws.OlePropertyGet("CurrentDirectory");
CurrentDirectory = CurrentDirectory + "\\Win32_Process.asp";
Variant fso = Variant::CreateObject("Scripting.FileSystemObject");
Variant         txtstream        =         fso.OleFunction("OpenTextFile",
OleVariant(CurrentDirectory), OleVariant(2), OleVariant(true), OleVariant(-2));

    txtstream.OleFunction("WriteLine",OleVariant(\"<html
xmlns='http://www.w3.org/1999/xhtml'>\"))");
    txtstream.OleFunction("WriteLine",OleVariant(\"<head>\"))");
    txtstream.OleFunction("WriteLine",OleVariant(\"<title>Win32_Process</title>
\"))");
    txtstream.OleFunction("WriteLine",OleVariant(\"</head>\"))");
```

```
txtstream.OleFunction("WriteLine",OleVariant(\"<body>\"))");
txtstream.OleFunction("WriteLine",OleVariant(\"<table                border='0'
Cellspacing='3' cellpadding = '3'>\"))");
txtstream.OleFunction("WriteLine",OleVariant(\"<%\"))");
```

Horizontal with no additional tags.

```
txtstream.OleFunction("WriteLine",OleVariant(\"Response.Write(\"<tr>\"    +
vbcrlf))");
for(int b = 0; b < w; b++)
{
    txtstream.OleFunction("WriteLine",OleVariant(\"Response.Write(\"<th
align='left' nowrap>" + Names[b] +"</th>\" + vbcrlf))");
}
txtstream.OleFunction("WriteLine",OleVariant(\"Response.Write(\"</tr>\"    +
vbcrlf))");
for(int a = 0; a < v; a++)
{
    txtstream.OleFunction("WriteLine",OleVariant(\"Response.Write(\"<tr>\"   +
vbcrlf))");
    for(int b = 0; b < w; b++)
    {
        txtstream.OleFunction("WriteLine",OleVariant(\"Response.Write(\"<td
style='font-family:Calibri,   Sans-Serif;font-size:   12px;color:navy;'   align='left'
nowrap='nowrap'>" + Values[a][b] +"</td>\" + vbcrlf))");
    }

txtstream.OleFunction("WriteLine",OleVariant(\"Response.Write(\"</tr>\"        +
vbcrlf))");
}
```

Horizontal with a Combobox.

```
txtstream.OleFunction("WriteLine",OleVariant(\"Response.Write(\"<tr>\"    +
vbcrlf))");
for(int b = 0; b < w; b++)
{
```

```
        txtstream.OleFunction("WriteLine",OleVariant(\"Response.Write(\"<th
align='left' nowrap>" + Names[b] +"</th>\" + vbcrlf))");
    }

    for(int a = 0; a < v; a++)
    {
        txtstream.OleFunction("WriteLine",OleVariant(\"Response.Write(\"<tr>\"  +
vbcrlf))");
        for(int b = 0; b < w; b++)
        {
            txtstream.OleFunction("WriteLine",OleVariant(\"Response.Write(\"<td
style='font-family:Calibri,   Sans-Serif;font-size:   12px;color:navy;'   align='left'
nowrap='true'><select><option value = '" + Values[a][b] +"'>" + Values[a][b]
+"</option></select></td>\" + vbcrlf))");
        }
        txtstream.OleFunction("WriteLine",OleVariant(\"Response.Write(\"</tr>\" +
vbcrlf))");
    }
```

Horizontal with a link.

```
    txtstream.OleFunction("WriteLine",OleVariant(\"Response.Write(\"<tr>\"       +
vbcrlf))");
    for(int b = 0; b < w; b++)
    {
        txtstream.OleFunction("WriteLine",OleVariant(\"Response.Write(\"<th
align='left' nowrap>" + Names[b] +"</th>\" + vbcrlf))");
    }


    for(int a = 0; a < v; a++)
    {
        txtstream.OleFunction("WriteLine",OleVariant(\"Response.Write(\"<tr>\"  +
vbcrlf))");
        for(int b = 0; b < w; b++)
        {

            txtstream.OleFunction("WriteLine",OleVariant(\"Response.Write(\"<td
style='font-family:Calibri,   Sans-Serif;font-size:   12px;color:navy;'   align='left'
```

```
nowrap='true'><a href='" + Values[a][b] +"'>" + Values[a][b] +"</a></td>\" +
vbcrlf))");
        }
        txtstream.OleFunction("WriteLine",OleVariant(\"Response.Write(\"</tr>\" +
vbcrlf))");
    }
```

Horizontal with a Listbox.

```
        txtstream.OleFunction("WriteLine",OleVariant(\"Response.Write(\"<tr>\"      +
vbcrlf))");
    for(int b = 0; b < w; b++)
    {
        txtstream.OleFunction("WriteLine",OleVariant(\"Response.Write(\"<th
align='left' nowrap>" + Names[b] +"</th>\" + vbcrlf))");
    }

    for(int a = 0; a < v; a++)
    {
        txtstream.OleFunction("WriteLine",OleVariant(\"Response.Write(\"<tr>\"   +
vbcrlf))");
        for(int b = 0; b < w; b++)
        {
            txtstream.OleFunction("WriteLine",OleVariant(\"Response.Write(\"<td
style='font-family:Calibri,     Sans-Serif;font-size:     12px;color:navy;'    align='left'
nowrap='true'><select  multiple><option  value  =  '"  +  Values[a][b]  +"'>"  +
Values[a][b] +"</option></select></td>\" + vbcrlf))");
        }
        txtstream.OleFunction("WriteLine",OleVariant(\"Response.Write(\"</tr>\" +
vbcrlf))");
    }
```

Horizontal with a textarea.

```
        txtstream.OleFunction("WriteLine",OleVariant(\"Response.Write(\"<tr>\"      +
vbcrlf))");
    for(int b = 0; b < w; b++)
    {
```

```
    txtstream.OleFunction("WriteLine",OleVariant(\"Response.Write(\"<th
align='left' nowrap>" + Names[b] +"</th>\" + vbcrlf))");
    }


    for(int a = 0; a < v; a++)
    {
        txtstream.OleFunction("WriteLine",OleVariant(\"Response.Write(\"<tr>\"   +
vbcrlf))");
        for(int b = 0; b < w; b++)
        {
            txtstream.OleFunction("WriteLine",OleVariant(\"Response.Write(\"<td
style='font-family:Calibri,   Sans-Serif;font-size:   12px;color:navy;'   align='left'
nowrap='true'><textarea>" + Values[a][b] +"</textarea></td>\" + vbcrlf))");
        }
        txtstream.OleFunction("WriteLine",OleVariant(\"Response.Write(\"</tr>\" +
vbcrlf))");
    }
```

Horizontal with a textbox.

```
    txtstream.OleFunction("WriteLine",OleVariant(\"Response.Write(\"<tr>\"      +
vbcrlf))");
    for(int b = 0; b < w; b++)
    {
        txtstream.OleFunction("WriteLine",OleVariant(\"Response.Write(\"<th
align='left' nowrap>" + Names[b] +"</th>\" + vbcrlf))");
    }


    for(int a = 0; a < v; a++)
    {
        txtstream.OleFunction("WriteLine",OleVariant(\"Response.Write(\"<tr>\"   +
vbcrlf))");
        for(int b = 0; b < w; b++)
        {
            txtstream.OleFunction("WriteLine",OleVariant(\"Response.Write(\"<td
style='font-family:Calibri,   Sans-Serif;font-size:   12px;color:navy;'   align='left'
nowrap='true'><input   type=text   value='" + Values[a][b] +"'></input></td>\"   +
vbcrlf))");
        }
```

```
        txtstream.OleFunction("WriteLine",OleVariant(\"Response.Write(\"</tr>\" +
vbcrlf))");
    }
```

Vertical with no additional tags.

```
    for(int b = 0; b < w; b++)
    {
```

```
txtstream.OleFunction("WriteLine",OleVariant(\"Response.Write(\"<tr><th
align='left' nowrap>" + Names[b] +"</th>\" + vbcrlf))");
        for(int a = 0; a < v; a++)
        {
            txtstream.OleFunction("WriteLine",OleVariant(\"Response.Write(\"<td
style='font-family:Calibri,    Sans-Serif;font-size:   12px;color:navy;'   align='left'
nowrap='nowrap'>" + Values[a][b] +"</td>\" + vbcrlf))");
        }
```

```
txtstream.OleFunction("WriteLine",OleVariant(\"Response.Write(\"</tr>\"           +
vbcrlf))");
    }
```

Vertical with a Combobox.

```
    for(int b = 0; b < w; b++)
    {
```

```
txtstream.OleFunction("WriteLine",OleVariant(\"Response.Write(\"<tr><th
align='left' nowrap>" + Names[b] +"</th>\" + vbcrlf))");
        for(int a = 0; a < v; a++)
        {
            txtstream.OleFunction("WriteLine",OleVariant(\"Response.Write(\"<td
style='font-family:Calibri,    Sans-Serif;font-size:   12px;color:navy;'   align='left'
nowrap='true'><select><option value = """ + Values[a][b] +""">" + Values[a][b]
+"</option></select></td>\" + vbcrlf))");
        }
```

```
txtstream.OleFunction("WriteLine",OleVariant(\"Response.Write(\"</tr>\"              +
vbcrlf))");
        }
```

Vertical with a link.

```
    for(int b = 0; b < w; b++)
    {

txtstream.OleFunction("WriteLine",OleVariant(\"Response.Write(\"<tr><th
align='left' nowrap>" + Names[b] +"</th>\" + vbcrlf))");
        for(int a = 0; a < v; a++)
        {
            txtstream.OleFunction("WriteLine",OleVariant(\"Response.Write(\"<td
style='font-family:Calibri,    Sans-Serif;font-size:    12px;color:navy;'    align='left'
nowrap='true'><a href='" + Values[a][b] +"'>" + Values[a][b] +"</a></td>\" +
vbcrlf))");
        }

txtstream.OleFunction("WriteLine",OleVariant(\"Response.Write(\"</tr>\"              +
vbcrlf))");
    }
```

Vertical with a Listbox.

```
    for(int b = 0; b < w; b++)
    {

txtstream.OleFunction("WriteLine",OleVariant(\"Response.Write(\"<tr><th
align='left' nowrap>" + Names[b] +"</th>\" + vbcrlf))");
        for(int a = 0; a < v; a++)
        {
            txtstream.OleFunction("WriteLine",OleVariant(\"Response.Write(\"<td
style='font-family:Calibri,    Sans-Serif;font-size:    12px;color:navy;'    align='left'
nowrap='true'><select multiple><option value = """ + Values[a][b] +""">" +
Values[a][b] +"</option></select></td>\" + vbcrlf))");
        }
```

```
        txtstream.OleFunction(“WriteLine”,OleVariant(\”Response.Write(\"</tr>\" +
vbcrlf))");
        }
```

Vertical with a textarea.

```
        for(int b = 0; b < w; b++)
        {

txtstream.OleFunction(“WriteLine”,OleVariant(\”Response.Write(\"<tr><th
align='left' nowrap>" + Names[b] +"</th>\" + vbcrlf))");
            for(int a = 0; a < v; a++)
            {
                txtstream.OleFunction(“WriteLine”,OleVariant(\”Response.Write(\"<td
style='font-family:Calibri,    Sans-Serif;font-size:    12px;color:navy;'    align='left'
nowrap='true'><textarea>" + Values[a][b] +"</textarea></td>\" + vbcrlf))");
            }

txtstream.OleFunction(“WriteLine”,OleVariant(\”Response.Write(\"</tr>\"           +
vbcrlf))");
        }
```

Vertical with a textbox.

```
        for(int b = 0; b < w; b++)
        {

txtstream.OleFunction(“WriteLine”,OleVariant(\”Response.Write(\"<tr><th
align='left' nowrap>" + Names[b] +"</th>\" + vbcrlf))");
            for(int a = 0; a < v; a++)
            {
                txtstream.OleFunction(“WriteLine”,OleVariant(\”Response.Write(\"<td
style='font-family:Calibri,    Sans-Serif;font-size:    12px;color:navy;'    align='left'
nowrap='true'><input type=text value="""" + Values[a][b] +"""></input></td>\" +
vbcrlf))");
            }
            txtstream.OleFunction(“WriteLine”,OleVariant(\”Response.Write(\"</tr>\" +
vbcrlf))");
        }
```

End Code

```
txtstream.OleFunction("WriteLine",OleVariant(\"%>\"))");
txtstream.OleFunction("WriteLine",OleVariant(\"</table>\"))");
txtstream.OleFunction("WriteLine",OleVariant(\"</body>\"))");
txtstream.OleFunction("WriteLine",OleVariant(\"</html>\"))");
txtstream.close();
```

ASP Tables

Begin Code

```
    Variant ws = Variant::CreateObject("WScript.Shell");
    String CurrentDirectory = ws.OlePropertyGet("CurrentDirectory");
    CurrentDirectory = CurrentDirectory + "\\Win32_Process.asp";
    Variant fso = Variant::CreateObject("Scripting.FileSystemObject");
    Variant        txtstream        =        fso.OleFunction("OpenTextFile",
OleVariant(CurrentDirectory), OleVariant(2), OleVariant(true), OleVariant(-2));


    txtstream.OleFunction("WriteLine",OleVariant(\"<html
xmlns='http://www.w3.org/1999/xhtml'>\"))");
    txtstream.OleFunction("WriteLine",OleVariant(\"<head>\"))");
    txtstream.OleFunction("WriteLine",OleVariant(\"<title>Win32_Process</title>
\"))");
    txtstream.OleFunction("WriteLine",OleVariant(\"</head>\"))");
    txtstream.OleFunction("WriteLine",OleVariant(\"<body>\"))");
    txtstream.OleFunction("WriteLine",OleVariant(\"<table                border='1'
Cellspacing='3' cellpadding = '3'>\"))");
    txtstream.OleFunction("WriteLine",OleVariant(\"<%\"))");
```

Horizontal with no additional tags.

```
    txtstream.OleFunction("WriteLine",OleVariant(\"Response.Write(\"<tr>\"    +
vbcrlf))");
    for(int b = 0; b < w; b++)
    {
```

```
        txtstream.OleFunction("WriteLine",OleVariant(\"Response.Write(\"<th
align='left' nowrap>" + Names[b] +"</th>\" + vbcrlf))");
        }
        txtstream.OleFunction("WriteLine",OleVariant(\"Response.Write(\"</tr>\"    +
vbcrlf))");
        for(int a = 0; a < v; a++)
        {
        txtstream.OleFunction("WriteLine",OleVariant(\"Response.Write(\"<tr>\"    +
vbcrlf))");
            for(int b = 0; b < w; b++)
            {
            txtstream.OleFunction("WriteLine",OleVariant(\"Response.Write(\"<td
style='font-family:Calibri,    Sans-Serif;font-size:    12px;color:navy;'    align='left'
nowrap='nowrap'>" + Values[a][b] +"</td>\" + vbcrlf))");
            }

txtstream.OleFunction("WriteLine",OleVariant(\"Response.Write(\"</tr>\"              +
vbcrlf))");
        }
```

Horizontal with a Combobox.

```
        txtstream.OleFunction("WriteLine",OleVariant(\"Response.Write(\"<tr>\"    +
vbcrlf))");
        for(int b = 0; b < w; b++)
        {
        txtstream.OleFunction("WriteLine",OleVariant(\"Response.Write(\"<th
align='left' nowrap>" + Names[b] +"</th>\" + vbcrlf))");
        }

        for(int a = 0; a < v; a++)
        {
        txtstream.OleFunction("WriteLine",OleVariant(\"Response.Write(\"<tr>\"    +
vbcrlf))");
            for(int b = 0; b < w; b++)
            {
            txtstream.OleFunction("WriteLine",OleVariant(\"Response.Write(\"<td
style='font-family:Calibri,    Sans-Serif;font-size:    12px;color:navy;'    align='left'
```

```
nowrap='true'><select><option value = '" + Values[a][b] +"'>" + Values[a][b]
+"</option></select></td>\" + vbcrlf))");
        }
        txtstream.OleFunction("WriteLine",OleVariant(\"Response.Write(\"</tr>\" +
vbcrlf))");
        }
```

Horizontal with a link.

```
        txtstream.OleFunction("WriteLine",OleVariant(\"Response.Write(\"<tr>\"       +
vbcrlf))");
        for(int b = 0; b < w; b++)
        {
        txtstream.OleFunction("WriteLine",OleVariant(\"Response.Write(\"<th
align='left' nowrap>" + Names[b] +"</th>\" + vbcrlf))");
        }


        for(int a = 0; a < v; a++)
        {
        txtstream.OleFunction("WriteLine",OleVariant(\"Response.Write(\"<tr>\"    +
vbcrlf))");
        for(int b = 0; b < w; b++)
        {

        txtstream.OleFunction("WriteLine",OleVariant(\"Response.Write(\"<td
style='font-family:Calibri,     Sans-Serif;font-size:     12px;color:navy;'    align='left'
nowrap='true'><a href='" + Values[a][b] +"'>" + Values[a][b] +"</a></td>\" +
vbcrlf))");
        }
        txtstream.OleFunction("WriteLine",OleVariant(\"Response.Write(\"</tr>\" +
vbcrlf))");
        }
```

Horizontal with a Listbox.

```
        txtstream.OleFunction("WriteLine",OleVariant(\"Response.Write(\"<tr>\"       +
vbcrlf))");
        for(int b = 0; b < w; b++)
        {
```

```
txtstream.OleFunction("WriteLine",OleVariant(\"Response.Write(\"<th
align='left' nowrap>" + Names[b] +"</th>\" + vbcrlf))");
    }

    for(int a = 0; a < v; a++)
    {
txtstream.OleFunction("WriteLine",OleVariant(\"Response.Write(\"<tr>\"  +
vbcrlf))");
        for(int b = 0; b < w; b++)
        {
        txtstream.OleFunction("WriteLine",OleVariant(\"Response.Write(\"<td
style='font-family:Calibri,   Sans-Serif;font-size:   12px;color:navy;'   align='left'
nowrap='true'><select  multiple><option  value  =  '"  +  Values[a][b]  +"'>"  +
Values[a][b] +"</option></select></td>\" + vbcrlf))");
        }
        txtstream.OleFunction("WriteLine",OleVariant(\"Response.Write(\"</tr>\" +
vbcrlf))");
    }
```

Horizontal with a textarea.

```
    txtstream.OleFunction("WriteLine",OleVariant(\"Response.Write(\"<tr>\"     +
vbcrlf))");
    for(int b = 0; b < w; b++)
    {
    txtstream.OleFunction("WriteLine",OleVariant(\"Response.Write(\"<th
align='left' nowrap>" + Names[b] +"</th>\" + vbcrlf))");
    }

    for(int a = 0; a < v; a++)
    {
    txtstream.OleFunction("WriteLine",OleVariant(\"Response.Write(\"<tr>\"   +
vbcrlf))");
        for(int b = 0; b < w; b++)
        {
```

```
          txtstream.OleFunction("WriteLine",OleVariant(\"Response.Write(\"<td
style='font-family:Calibri,   Sans-Serif;font-size:   12px;color:navy;'   align='left'
nowrap='true'><textarea>" + Values[a][b] +"</textarea></td>\" + vbcrlf))");
          }
          txtstream.OleFunction("WriteLine",OleVariant(\"Response.Write(\"</tr>\" +
vbcrlf))");
       }
```

Horizontal with a textbox.

```
       txtstream.OleFunction("WriteLine",OleVariant(\"Response.Write(\"<tr>\"      +
vbcrlf))");
      for(int b = 0; b < w; b++)
      {
          txtstream.OleFunction("WriteLine",OleVariant(\"Response.Write(\"<th
align='left' nowrap>" + Names[b] +"</th>\" + vbcrlf))");
      }


      for(int a = 0; a < v; a++)
      {
          txtstream.OleFunction("WriteLine",OleVariant(\"Response.Write(\"<tr>\"   +
vbcrlf))");
          for(int b = 0; b < w; b++)
          {
            txtstream.OleFunction("WriteLine",OleVariant(\"Response.Write(\"<td
style='font-family:Calibri,   Sans-Serif;font-size:   12px;color:navy;'   align='left'
nowrap='true'><input  type=text  value='"  +  Values[a][b]  +"'></input></td>\"   +
vbcrlf))");
          }
          txtstream.OleFunction("WriteLine",OleVariant(\"Response.Write(\"</tr>\" +
vbcrlf))");
      }
```

Vertical with no additional tags.

```
      for(int b = 0; b < w; b++)
      {
```

```
txtstream.OleFunction("WriteLine",OleVariant(\"Response.Write(\"<tr><th
align='left' nowrap>" + Names[b] +"</th>\" + vbcrlf))");
        for(int a = 0; a < v; a++)
        {
            txtstream.OleFunction("WriteLine",OleVariant(\"Response.Write(\"<td
style='font-family:Calibri,    Sans-Serif;font-size:    12px;color:navy;'    align='left'
nowrap='nowrap'>" + Values[a][b] +"</td>\" + vbcrlf))");
        }

txtstream.OleFunction("WriteLine",OleVariant(\"Response.Write(\"</tr>\"            +
vbcrlf))");
    }
```

Vertical with a Combobox.

```
    for(int b = 0; b < w; b++)
    {

txtstream.OleFunction("WriteLine",OleVariant(\"Response.Write(\"<tr><th
align='left' nowrap>" + Names[b] +"</th>\" + vbcrlf))");
        for(int a = 0; a < v; a++)
        {
            txtstream.OleFunction("WriteLine",OleVariant(\"Response.Write(\"<td
style='font-family:Calibri,    Sans-Serif;font-size:    12px;color:navy;'    align='left'
nowrap='true'><select><option value = "'" + Values[a][b] +"'">" + Values[a][b]
+"</option></select></td>\" + vbcrlf))");
        }

txtstream.OleFunction("WriteLine",OleVariant(\"Response.Write(\"</tr>\"            +
vbcrlf))");
    }
```

Vertical with a link.

```
    for(int b = 0; b < w; b++)
    {
```

```
txtstream.OleFunction("WriteLine",OleVariant(\"Response.Write(\"<tr><th
align='left' nowrap>" + Names[b] +"</th>\" + vbcrlf))");
        for(int a = 0; a < v; a++)
        {
            txtstream.OleFunction("WriteLine",OleVariant(\"Response.Write(\"<td
style='font-family:Calibri,  Sans-Serif;font-size:  12px;color:navy;'  align='left'
nowrap='true'><a href='" + Values[a][b] +"'>" + Values[a][b] +"</a></td>\" +
vbcrlf))");
        }

txtstream.OleFunction("WriteLine",OleVariant(\"Response.Write(\"</tr>\"            +
vbcrlf))");
    }
```

Vertical with a Listbox.

```
    for(int b = 0; b < w; b++)
    {

txtstream.OleFunction("WriteLine",OleVariant(\"Response.Write(\"<tr><th
align='left' nowrap>" + Names[b] +"</th>\" + vbcrlf))");
        for(int a = 0; a < v; a++)
        {
            txtstream.OleFunction("WriteLine",OleVariant(\"Response.Write(\"<td
style='font-family:Calibri,  Sans-Serif;font-size:  12px;color:navy;'  align='left'
nowrap='true'><select multiple><option value = "'" + Values[a][b] +"'">" +
Values[a][b] +"</option></select></td>\" + vbcrlf))");
        }
        txtstream.OleFunction("WriteLine",OleVariant(\"Response.Write(\"</tr>\" +
vbcrlf))");
    }
```

Vertical with a textarea.

```
    for(int b = 0; b < w; b++)
    {

txtstream.OleFunction("WriteLine",OleVariant(\"Response.Write(\"<tr><th
align='left' nowrap>" + Names[b] +"</th>\" + vbcrlf))");
        for(int a = 0; a < v; a++)
```

```
        {
            txtstream.OleFunction("WriteLine",OleVariant(\"Response.Write(\"<td
style='font-family:Calibri,    Sans-Serif;font-size:   12px;color:navy;'   align='left'
nowrap='true'><textarea>" + Values[a][b] +"</textarea></td>\" + vbcrlf))");
        }

txtstream.OleFunction("WriteLine",OleVariant(\"Response.Write(\"</tr>\"          +
vbcrlf))");
    }
```

Vertical with a textbox.

```
    for(int b = 0; b < w; b++)
    {

txtstream.OleFunction("WriteLine",OleVariant(\"Response.Write(\"<tr><th
align='left' nowrap>" + Names[b] +"</th>\" + vbcrlf))");
        for(int a = 0; a < v; a++)
        {
            txtstream.OleFunction("WriteLine",OleVariant(\"Response.Write(\"<td
style='font-family:Calibri,    Sans-Serif;font-size:   12px;color:navy;'   align='left'
nowrap='true'><input type=text value="""" + Values[a][b] +""""></input></td>\" +
vbcrlf))");
        }
        txtstream.OleFunction("WriteLine",OleVariant(\"Response.Write(\"</tr>\" +
vbcrlf))");
    }
```

End Code

```
        txtstream.OleFunction("WriteLine",OleVariant(\"%>\"))");
        txtstream.OleFunction("WriteLine",OleVariant(\"</table>\"))");
        txtstream.OleFunction("WriteLine",OleVariant(\"</body>\"))");
        txtstream.OleFunction("WriteLine",OleVariant(\"</html>\"))");
        txtstream.close();
```

Begin Code

```
    Variant ws = Variant::CreateObject("WScript.Shell");
    String CurrentDirectory = ws.OlePropertyGet("CurrentDirectory");
    CurrentDirectory = CurrentDirectory + "\\Win32_Process.aspx";
    Variant fso = Variant::CreateObject("Scripting.FileSystemObject");
    Variant        txtstream        =        fso.OleFunction("OpenTextFile",
OleVariant(CurrentDirectory), OleVariant(2), OleVariant(true), OleVariant(-2));

    txtstream.OleFunction("WriteLine",OleVariant(\"<!DOCTYPE html PUBLIC ""-
//W3C//DTD        XHTML        1.0        Transitional//EN""
""http://www.w3.org/TR/xhtml1/DTD/xhtml1-transitional.dtd"">\"))");
    txtstream.OleFunction("WriteLine",OleVariant(\"<html
xmlns='http://www.w3.org/1999/xhtml'>\"))");
    txtstream.OleFunction("WriteLine",OleVariant(\"<head>\"))");
    txtstream.OleFunction("WriteLine",OleVariant(\"<title>Win32_Process</title>
\"))");
    txtstream.OleFunction("WriteLine",OleVariant(\"</head>\"))");
    txtstream.OleFunction("WriteLine",OleVariant(\"<body>\"))");
    txtstream.OleFunction("WriteLine",OleVariant(\"<table        border='0'
Cellspacing='3' cellpadding = '3'>\"))");
    txtstream.OleFunction("WriteLine",OleVariant(\"<%\"))");
```

Horizontal with no additional tags.

```
    txtstream.OleFunction("WriteLine",OleVariant(\"Response.Write(\"<tr>\"    +
vbcrlf))");
    for(int b = 0; b < w; b++)
    {
        txtstream.OleFunction("WriteLine",OleVariant(\"Response.Write(\"<th
align='left' nowrap>" + Names[b] +"</th>\" + vbcrlf))");
    }
    txtstream.OleFunction("WriteLine",OleVariant(\"Response.Write(\"</tr>\"    +
vbcrlf))");
    for(int a = 0; a < v; a++)
    {
        txtstream.OleFunction("WriteLine",OleVariant(\"Response.Write(\"<tr>\"  +
vbcrlf))");
        for(int b = 0; b < w; b++)
        {
            txtstream.OleFunction("WriteLine",OleVariant(\"Response.Write(\"<td
style='font-family:Calibri,    Sans-Serif;font-size:    12px;color:navy;'    align='left'
nowrap='nowrap'>" + Values[a][b] +"</td>\" + vbcrlf))");
        }

txtstream.OleFunction("WriteLine",OleVariant(\"Response.Write(\"</tr>\"         +
vbcrlf))");
    }
```

Horizontal with a Combobox.

```
    txtstream.OleFunction("WriteLine",OleVariant(\"Response.Write(\"<tr>\"    +
vbcrlf))");
    for(int b = 0; b < w; b++)
    {
        txtstream.OleFunction("WriteLine",OleVariant(\"Response.Write(\"<th
align='left' nowrap>" + Names[b] +"</th>\" + vbcrlf))");
    }

    for(int a = 0; a < v; a++)
```

```
    {
        txtstream.OleFunction("WriteLine",OleVariant(\"Response.Write(\"<tr>\"   +
vbcrlf))");
        for(int b = 0; b < w; b++)
        {
            txtstream.OleFunction("WriteLine",OleVariant(\"Response.Write(\"<td
style='font-family:Calibri,    Sans-Serif;font-size:    12px;color:navy;'   align='left'
nowrap='true'><select><option value = '"  +  Values[a][b]  +"'>"  +  Values[a][b]
+"</option></select></td>\" + vbcrlf))");
        }
        txtstream.OleFunction("WriteLine",OleVariant(\"Response.Write(\"</tr>\"  +
vbcrlf))");
    }
```

Horizontal with a link.

```
        txtstream.OleFunction("WriteLine",OleVariant(\"Response.Write(\"<tr>\"       +
vbcrlf))");
        for(int b = 0; b < w; b++)
        {
            txtstream.OleFunction("WriteLine",OleVariant(\"Response.Write(\"<th
align='left' nowrap>" + Names[b] +"</th>\" + vbcrlf))");
        }


        for(int a = 0; a < v; a++)
        {
            txtstream.OleFunction("WriteLine",OleVariant(\"Response.Write(\"<tr>\"   +
vbcrlf))");
            for(int b = 0; b < w; b++)
            {

                txtstream.OleFunction("WriteLine",OleVariant(\"Response.Write(\"<td
style='font-family:Calibri,    Sans-Serif;font-size:    12px;color:navy;'   align='left'
nowrap='true'><a  href='"  +  Values[a][b]  +"'>"  +  Values[a][b]  +"</a></td>\"  +
vbcrlf))");
            }
            txtstream.OleFunction("WriteLine",OleVariant(\"Response.Write(\"</tr>\"  +
vbcrlf))");
        }
```

Horizontal with a Listbox.

```
        txtstream.OleFunction("WriteLine",OleVariant(\"Response.Write(\"<tr>\"      +
vbcrlf))");
     for(int b = 0; b < w; b++)
     {
        txtstream.OleFunction("WriteLine",OleVariant(\"Response.Write(\"<th
align='left' nowrap>" + Names[b] +"</th>\" + vbcrlf))");
     }

     for(int a = 0; a < v; a++)
     {
        txtstream.OleFunction("WriteLine",OleVariant(\"Response.Write(\"<tr>\"   +
vbcrlf))");
         for(int b = 0; b < w; b++)
         {
            txtstream.OleFunction("WriteLine",OleVariant(\"Response.Write(\"<td
style='font-family:Calibri,    Sans-Serif;font-size:   12px;color:navy;'   align='left'
nowrap='true'><select  multiple><option  value  =  '"  +  Values[a][b]  +"'>"  +
Values[a][b] +"</option></select></td>\" + vbcrlf))");
         }
         txtstream.OleFunction("WriteLine",OleVariant(\"Response.Write(\"</tr>\" +
vbcrlf))");
     }
```

Horizontal with a textarea.

```
        txtstream.OleFunction("WriteLine",OleVariant(\"Response.Write(\"<tr>\"      +
vbcrlf))");
     for(int b = 0; b < w; b++)
     {
        txtstream.OleFunction("WriteLine",OleVariant(\"Response.Write(\"<th
align='left' nowrap>" + Names[b] +"</th>\" + vbcrlf))");
     }

     for(int a = 0; a < v; a++)
```

```
        {
            txtstream.OleFunction("WriteLine",OleVariant(\"Response.Write(\"<tr>\"   +
vbcrlf))");
            for(int b = 0; b < w; b++)
            {
                txtstream.OleFunction("WriteLine",OleVariant(\"Response.Write(\"<td
style='font-family:Calibri,   Sans-Serif;font-size:   12px;color:navy;'   align='left'
nowrap='true'><textarea>" + Values[a][b] +"</textarea></td>\" + vbcrlf))");
            }
            txtstream.OleFunction("WriteLine",OleVariant(\"Response.Write(\"</tr>\" +
vbcrlf))");
        }
```

Horizontal with a textbox.

```
        txtstream.OleFunction("WriteLine",OleVariant(\"Response.Write(\"<tr>\"      +
vbcrlf))");
        for(int b = 0; b < w; b++)
        {
            txtstream.OleFunction("WriteLine",OleVariant(\"Response.Write(\"<th
align='left' nowrap>" + Names[b] +"</th>\" + vbcrlf))");
        }


        for(int a = 0; a < v; a++)
        {
            txtstream.OleFunction("WriteLine",OleVariant(\"Response.Write(\"<tr>\"   +
vbcrlf))");
            for(int b = 0; b < w; b++)
            {
                txtstream.OleFunction("WriteLine",OleVariant(\"Response.Write(\"<td
style='font-family:Calibri,   Sans-Serif;font-size:   12px;color:navy;'   align='left'
nowrap='true'><input  type=text  value='" + Values[a][b]  +"'></input></td>\"  +
vbcrlf))");
            }
            txtstream.OleFunction("WriteLine",OleVariant(\"Response.Write(\"</tr>\" +
vbcrlf))");
        }
```

Vertical with no additional tags.

```
        for(int b = 0; b < w; b++)
        {

txtstream.OleFunction("WriteLine",OleVariant(\"Response.Write(\"<tr><th
align='left' nowrap>" + Names[b] +"</th>\" + vbcrlf))");
            for(int a = 0; a < v; a++)
            {
                txtstream.OleFunction("WriteLine",OleVariant(\"Response.Write(\"<td
style='font-family:Calibri,   Sans-Serif;font-size:   12px;color:navy;'   align='left'
nowrap='nowrap'>" + Values[a][b] +"</td>\" + vbcrlf))");
            }

txtstream.OleFunction("WriteLine",OleVariant(\"Response.Write(\"</tr>\"            +
vbcrlf))");
        }
```

Vertical with a Combobox.

```
        for(int b = 0; b < w; b++)
        {

txtstream.OleFunction("WriteLine",OleVariant(\"Response.Write(\"<tr><th
align='left' nowrap>" + Names[b] +"</th>\" + vbcrlf))");
            for(int a = 0; a < v; a++)
            {
                txtstream.OleFunction("WriteLine",OleVariant(\"Response.Write(\"<td
style='font-family:Calibri,   Sans-Serif;font-size:   12px;color:navy;'   align='left'
nowrap='true'><select><option value = '""'" + Values[a][b] +"'"">" + Values[a][b]
+"</option></select></td>\" + vbcrlf))");
            }

txtstream.OleFunction("WriteLine",OleVariant(\"Response.Write(\"</tr>\"            +
vbcrlf))");
        }
```

Vertical with a link.

```
    for(int b = 0; b < w; b++)
    {

txtstream.OleFunction("WriteLine",OleVariant(\"Response.Write(\"<tr><th
align='left' nowrap>" + Names[b] +"</th>\" + vbcrlf))");
        for(int a = 0; a < v; a++)
        {
            txtstream.OleFunction("WriteLine",OleVariant(\"Response.Write(\"<td
style='font-family:Calibri,    Sans-Serif;font-size:   12px;color:navy;'   align='left'
nowrap='true'><a  href='"  +  Values[a][b]  +"'>"  +  Values[a][b]  +"</a></td>\"  +
vbcrlf))");
        }

txtstream.OleFunction("WriteLine",OleVariant(\"Response.Write(\"</tr>\"            +
vbcrlf))");
    }
```

Vertical with a Listbox.

```
    for(int b = 0; b < w; b++)
    {

txtstream.OleFunction("WriteLine",OleVariant(\"Response.Write(\"<tr><th
align='left' nowrap>" + Names[b] +"</th>\" + vbcrlf))");
        for(int a = 0; a < v; a++)
        {
            txtstream.OleFunction("WriteLine",OleVariant(\"Response.Write(\"<td
style='font-family:Calibri,    Sans-Serif;font-size:   12px;color:navy;'   align='left'
nowrap='true'><select  multiple><option value  =  "'"  +  Values[a][b]  +"'">"  +
Values[a][b] +"</option></select></td>\" + vbcrlf))");
        }
            txtstream.OleFunction("WriteLine",OleVariant(\"Response.Write(\"</tr>\" +
vbcrlf))");
    }
```

Vertical with a textarea.

```
    for(int b = 0; b < w; b++)
    {

txtstream.OleFunction("WriteLine",OleVariant(\"Response.Write(\"<tr><th
align='left' nowrap>" + Names[b] +"</th>\" + vbcrlf))");
        for(int a = 0; a < v; a++)
        {
            txtstream.OleFunction("WriteLine",OleVariant(\"Response.Write(\"<td
style='font-family:Calibri,    Sans-Serif;font-size:    12px;color:navy;'    align='left'
nowrap='true'><textarea>" + Values[a][b] +"</textarea></td>\" + vbcrlf))");
        }

txtstream.OleFunction("WriteLine",OleVariant(\"Response.Write(\"</tr>\"            +
vbcrlf))");
    }
```

Vertical with a textbox.

```
    for(int b = 0; b < w; b++)
    {

txtstream.OleFunction("WriteLine",OleVariant(\"Response.Write(\"<tr><th
align='left' nowrap>" + Names[b] +"</th>\" + vbcrlf))");
        for(int a = 0; a < v; a++)
        {
            txtstream.OleFunction("WriteLine",OleVariant(\"Response.Write(\"<td
style='font-family:Calibri,    Sans-Serif;font-size:    12px;color:navy;'    align='left'
nowrap='true'><input type=text value="""" + Values[a][b] +"""""></input></td>\" +
vbcrlf))");
        }
        txtstream.OleFunction("WriteLine",OleVariant(\"Response.Write(\"</tr>\" +
vbcrlf))");
    }
```

End Code

```
txtstream.OleFunction("WriteLine",OleVariant(\"%>\"))");
txtstream.OleFunction("WriteLine",OleVariant(\"</table>\"))");
txtstream.OleFunction("WriteLine",OleVariant(\"</body>\"))");
txtstream.OleFunction("WriteLine",OleVariant(\"</html>\"))");
txtstream.close();
```

ASPX Tables

Begin Code

```
Variant ws = Variant::CreateObject("WScript.Shell");
String CurrentDirectory = ws.OlePropertyGet("CurrentDirectory");
CurrentDirectory = CurrentDirectory + "\\Win32_Process.aspx";
Variant fso = Variant::CreateObject("Scripting.FileSystemObject");
Variant         txtstream         =         fso.OleFunction("OpenTextFile",
OleVariant(CurrentDirectory), OleVariant(2), OleVariant(true), OleVariant(-2));

txtstream.OleFunction("WriteLine",OleVariant(\"<!DOCTYPE html PUBLIC ""-
//W3C//DTD         XHTML         1.0         Transitional//EN""
""http://www.w3.org/TR/xhtml1/DTD/xhtml1-transitional.dtd""">\"))");
txtstream.OleFunction("WriteLine",OleVariant(\"<html
xmlns='http://www.w3.org/1999/xhtml'>\"))");
txtstream.OleFunction("WriteLine",OleVariant(\"<head>\"))");
txtstream.OleFunction("WriteLine",OleVariant(\"<title>Win32_Process</title>
\"))");
txtstream.OleFunction("WriteLine",OleVariant(\"</head>\"))");
```

```
txtstream.OleFunction("WriteLine",OleVariant(\"<body>\"))");
txtstream.OleFunction("WriteLine",OleVariant(\"<table            border='1'
Cellspacing='3' cellpadding = '3'>\"))");
txtstream.OleFunction("WriteLine",OleVariant(\"<%\"))");
```

Horizontal with no additional tags.

```
txtstream.OleFunction("WriteLine",OleVariant(\"Response.Write(\"<tr>\"    +
vbcrlf))");
    for(int b = 0; b < w; b++)
    {
        txtstream.OleFunction("WriteLine",OleVariant(\"Response.Write(\"<th
align='left' nowrap>" + Names[b] +"</th>\" + vbcrlf))");
    }
    txtstream.OleFunction("WriteLine",OleVariant(\"Response.Write(\"</tr>\"    +
vbcrlf))");
    for(int a = 0; a < v; a++)
    {
        txtstream.OleFunction("WriteLine",OleVariant(\"Response.Write(\"<tr>\"  +
vbcrlf))");
        for(int b = 0; b < w; b++)
        {
            txtstream.OleFunction("WriteLine",OleVariant(\"Response.Write(\"<td
style='font-family:Calibri,   Sans-Serif;font-size:   12px;color:navy;'   align='left'
nowrap='nowrap'>" + Values[a][b] +"</td>\" + vbcrlf))");
        }

txtstream.OleFunction("WriteLine",OleVariant(\"Response.Write(\"</tr>\"         +
vbcrlf))");
    }
```

Horizontal with a Combobox.

```
txtstream.OleFunction("WriteLine",OleVariant(\"Response.Write(\"<tr>\"    +
vbcrlf))");
    for(int b = 0; b < w; b++)
    {
```

```
        txtstream.OleFunction("WriteLine",OleVariant(\"Response.Write(\"<th
align='left' nowrap>" + Names[b] +"</th>\" + vbcrlf))");
        }

    for(int a = 0; a < v; a++)
    {
        txtstream.OleFunction("WriteLine",OleVariant(\"Response.Write(\"<tr>\"    +
vbcrlf))");
        for(int b = 0; b < w; b++)
        {
            txtstream.OleFunction("WriteLine",OleVariant(\"Response.Write(\"<td
style='font-family:Calibri,    Sans-Serif;font-size:    12px;color:navy;'    align='left'
nowrap='true'><select><option value = '"  + Values[a][b] +"'>" + Values[a][b]
+"</option></select></td>\" + vbcrlf))");
        }
        txtstream.OleFunction("WriteLine",OleVariant(\"Response.Write(\"</tr>\" +
vbcrlf))");
    }
```

Horizontal with a link.

```
    txtstream.OleFunction("WriteLine",OleVariant(\"Response.Write(\"<tr>\"      +
vbcrlf))");
    for(int b = 0; b < w; b++)
    {
        txtstream.OleFunction("WriteLine",OleVariant(\"Response.Write(\"<th
align='left' nowrap>" + Names[b] +"</th>\" + vbcrlf))");
    }


    for(int a = 0; a < v; a++)
    {
        txtstream.OleFunction("WriteLine",OleVariant(\"Response.Write(\"<tr>\"    +
vbcrlf))");
        for(int b = 0; b < w; b++)
        {

            txtstream.OleFunction("WriteLine",OleVariant(\"Response.Write(\"<td
style='font-family:Calibri,    Sans-Serif;font-size:    12px;color:navy;'    align='left'
```

```
nowrap='true'><a  href='''  +  Values[a][b]  +"'>"  +  Values[a][b]  +"</a></td>\"  +
vbcrlf))");
        }
        txtstream.OleFunction("WriteLine",OleVariant(\"Response.Write(\"</tr>\"  +
vbcrlf))");
    }
```

Horizontal with a Listbox.

```
    txtstream.OleFunction("WriteLine",OleVariant(\"Response.Write(\"<tr>\"        +
vbcrlf))");
    for(int b = 0; b < w; b++)
    {
        txtstream.OleFunction("WriteLine",OleVariant(\"Response.Write(\"<th
align='left' nowrap>" + Names[b] +"</th>\" + vbcrlf))");
    }

    for(int a = 0; a < v; a++)
    {
        txtstream.OleFunction("WriteLine",OleVariant(\"Response.Write(\"<tr>\"   +
vbcrlf))");
        for(int b = 0; b < w; b++)
        {
            txtstream.OleFunction("WriteLine",OleVariant(\"Response.Write(\"<td
style='font-family:Calibri,    Sans-Serif;font-size:    12px;color:navy;'    align='left'
nowrap='true'><select    multiple><option    value    =    '''    +    Values[a][b]    +"'>"    +
Values[a][b] +"</option></select></td>\" + vbcrlf))");
        }
        txtstream.OleFunction("WriteLine",OleVariant(\"Response.Write(\"</tr>\"  +
vbcrlf))");
    }
```

Horizontal with a textarea.

```
    txtstream.OleFunction("WriteLine",OleVariant(\"Response.Write(\"<tr>\"        +
vbcrlf))");
    for(int b = 0; b < w; b++)
    {
```

```
        txtstream.OleFunction("WriteLine",OleVariant(\"Response.Write(\"<th
align='left' nowrap>" + Names[b] +"</th>\" + vbcrlf))");
    }


    for(int a = 0; a < v; a++)
    {
        txtstream.OleFunction("WriteLine",OleVariant(\"Response.Write(\"<tr>\"   +
vbcrlf))");
        for(int b = 0; b < w; b++)
        {
            txtstream.OleFunction("WriteLine",OleVariant(\"Response.Write(\"<td
style='font-family:Calibri,  Sans-Serif;font-size:  12px;color:navy;'  align='left'
nowrap='true'><textarea>" + Values[a][b] +"</textarea></td>\" + vbcrlf))");
        }
        txtstream.OleFunction("WriteLine",OleVariant(\"Response.Write(\"</tr>\" +
vbcrlf))");
    }
```

Horizontal with a textbox.

```
        txtstream.OleFunction("WriteLine",OleVariant(\"Response.Write(\"<tr>\"     +
vbcrlf))");
    for(int b = 0; b < w; b++)
    {
        txtstream.OleFunction("WriteLine",OleVariant(\"Response.Write(\"<th
align='left' nowrap>" + Names[b] +"</th>\" + vbcrlf))");
    }


    for(int a = 0; a < v; a++)
    {
        txtstream.OleFunction("WriteLine",OleVariant(\"Response.Write(\"<tr>\"   +
vbcrlf))");
        for(int b = 0; b < w; b++)
        {
            txtstream.OleFunction("WriteLine",OleVariant(\"Response.Write(\"<td
style='font-family:Calibri,  Sans-Serif;font-size:  12px;color:navy;'  align='left'
nowrap='true'><input type=text value='" + Values[a][b] +"'></input></td>\"   +
vbcrlf))");
        }
```

```
        txtstream.OleFunction("WriteLine",OleVariant(\"Response.Write(\"</tr>\" +
vbcrlf))");
    }
```

Vertical with no additional tags.

```
    for(int b = 0; b < w; b++)
    {

txtstream.OleFunction("WriteLine",OleVariant(\"Response.Write(\"<tr><th
align='left' nowrap>" + Names[b] +"</th>\" + vbcrlf))");
        for(int a = 0; a < v; a++)
        {
            txtstream.OleFunction("WriteLine",OleVariant(\"Response.Write(\"<td
style='font-family:Calibri,    Sans-Serif;font-size:    12px;color:navy;'    align='left'
nowrap='nowrap'>" + Values[a][b] +"</td>\" + vbcrlf))");
        }

txtstream.OleFunction("WriteLine",OleVariant(\"Response.Write(\"</tr>\"              +
vbcrlf))");
    }
```

Vertical with a Combobox.

```
    for(int b = 0; b < w; b++)
    {

txtstream.OleFunction("WriteLine",OleVariant(\"Response.Write(\"<tr><th
align='left' nowrap>" + Names[b] +"</th>\" + vbcrlf))");
        for(int a = 0; a < v; a++)
        {
            txtstream.OleFunction("WriteLine",OleVariant(\"Response.Write(\"<td
style='font-family:Calibri,    Sans-Serif;font-size:    12px;color:navy;'    align='left'
nowrap='true'><select><option value = "'" + Values[a][b] +"'">" + Values[a][b]
+"</option></select></td>\" + vbcrlf))");
        }
```

```
txtstream.OleFunction("WriteLine",OleVariant(\"Response.Write(\"</tr>\"          +
vbcrlf))");
        }
```

Vertical with a link.

```
        for(int b = 0; b < w; b++)
        {

txtstream.OleFunction("WriteLine",OleVariant(\"Response.Write(\"<tr><th
align='left' nowrap>" + Names[b] +"</th>\" + vbcrlf))");
            for(int a = 0; a < v; a++)
            {
                txtstream.OleFunction("WriteLine",OleVariant(\"Response.Write(\"<td
style='font-family:Calibri,    Sans-Serif;font-size:    12px;color:navy;'    align='left'
nowrap='true'><a   href='"   +   Values[a][b]   +"'>"   +   Values[a][b]   +"</a></td>\"   +
vbcrlf))");
            }

txtstream.OleFunction("WriteLine",OleVariant(\"Response.Write(\"</tr>\"          +
vbcrlf))");
        }
```

Vertical with a Listbox.

```
        for(int b = 0; b < w; b++)
        {

txtstream.OleFunction("WriteLine",OleVariant(\"Response.Write(\"<tr><th
align='left' nowrap>" + Names[b] +"</th>\" + vbcrlf))");
            for(int a = 0; a < v; a++)
            {
                txtstream.OleFunction("WriteLine",OleVariant(\"Response.Write(\"<td
style='font-family:Calibri,    Sans-Serif;font-size:    12px;color:navy;'    align='left'
nowrap='true'><select  multiple><option  value  =  "'"  +  Values[a][b]  +"'">"  +
Values[a][b] +"</option></select></td>\" + vbcrlf))");
            }
```

```
        txtstream.OleFunction("WriteLine",OleVariant(\"Response.Write(\"</tr>\" +
vbcrlf))");
    }
```

Vertical with a textarea.

```
    for(int b = 0; b < w; b++)
    {

txtstream.OleFunction("WriteLine",OleVariant(\"Response.Write(\"<tr><th
align='left' nowrap>" + Names[b] +"</th>\" + vbcrlf))");
        for(int a = 0; a < v; a++)
        {
            txtstream.OleFunction("WriteLine",OleVariant(\"Response.Write(\"<td
style='font-family:Calibri,    Sans-Serif;font-size:    12px;color:navy;'    align='left'
nowrap='true'><textarea>" + Values[a][b] +"</textarea></td>\" + vbcrlf))");
        }

txtstream.OleFunction("WriteLine",OleVariant(\"Response.Write(\"</tr>\"              +
vbcrlf))");
    }
```

Vertical with a textbox.

```
    for(int b = 0; b < w; b++)
    {

txtstream.OleFunction("WriteLine",OleVariant(\"Response.Write(\"<tr><th
align='left' nowrap>" + Names[b] +"</th>\" + vbcrlf))");
        for(int a = 0; a < v; a++)
        {
            txtstream.OleFunction("WriteLine",OleVariant(\"Response.Write(\"<td
style='font-family:Calibri,    Sans-Serif;font-size:    12px;color:navy;'    align='left'
nowrap='true'><input type=text value="'"" + Values[a][b] +"'"'"></input></td>\" +
vbcrlf))");
        }
        txtstream.OleFunction("WriteLine",OleVariant(\"Response.Write(\"</tr>\" +
vbcrlf))");
    }
```

End Code

```
txtstream.OleFunction("WriteLine",OleVariant(\"%>\"))");
txtstream.OleFunction("WriteLine",OleVariant(\"</table>\"))");
txtstream.OleFunction("WriteLine",OleVariant(\"</body>\"))");
txtstream.OleFunction("WriteLine",OleVariant(\"</html>\"))");
txtstream.close();
```

HTA Reports

Begin Code

```
Variant ws = Variant::CreateObject("WScript.Shell");
String CurrentDirectory = ws.OlePropertyGet("CurrentDirectory");
CurrentDirectory = CurrentDirectory + "\\Win32_Process.hta";
Variant fso = Variant::CreateObject("Scripting.FileSystemObject");
Variant          txtstream          =          fso.OleFunction("OpenTextFile",
OleVariant(CurrentDirectory), OleVariant(2), OleVariant(true), OleVariant(-2));

txtstream.OleFunction("WriteLine",OleVariant(\"<html
xmlns='http://www.w3.org/1999/xhtml'>\"))");
txtstream.OleFunction("WriteLine",OleVariant(\"<head>\"))");
txtstream.OleFunction("WriteLine",OleVariant(\"<HTA:APPLICATION ");
txtstream.OleFunction("WriteLine",OleVariant(\"ID = ""Process"" ");
txtstream.OleFunction("WriteLine",OleVariant(\"APPLICATIONNAME          =
""Process"" ");
txtstream.OleFunction("WriteLine",OleVariant(\"SCROLL = ""yes"" ");
txtstream.OleFunction("WriteLine",OleVariant(\"SINGLEINSTANCE  =  ""yes""
");
txtstream.OleFunction("WriteLine",OleVariant(\"WINDOWSTATE          =
""maximize"" >\"))");
txtstream.OleFunction("WriteLine",OleVariant(\"</head>\"))");
txtstream.OleFunction("WriteLine",OleVariant(\"<body>\"))");
txtstream.OleFunction("WriteLine",OleVariant(\"<table          border='0'
Cellspacing='3' cellpadding = '3'>\"))");
```

Horizontal with no additional tags.

```
txtstream.OleFunction("WriteLine",OleVariant(\"Response.Write(\"<tr>\"      +
vbcrlf))");
    for(int b = 0; b < w; b++)
    {
        txtstream.OleFunction("WriteLine",OleVariant(\"Response.Write(\"<th
align='left' nowrap>" + Names[b] +"</th>\" + vbcrlf))");
    }
    txtstream.OleFunction("WriteLine",OleVariant(\"Response.Write(\"</tr>\"      +
vbcrlf))");
    for(int a = 0; a < v; a++)
    {
        txtstream.OleFunction("WriteLine",OleVariant(\"Response.Write(\"<tr>\"  +
vbcrlf))");
        for(int b = 0; b < w; b++)
        {
            txtstream.OleFunction("WriteLine",OleVariant(\"Response.Write(\"<td
style='font-family:Calibri,    Sans-Serif;font-size:    12px;color:navy;'    align='left'
nowrap='nowrap'>" + Values[a][b] +"</td>\" + vbcrlf))");
        }

txtstream.OleFunction("WriteLine",OleVariant(\"Response.Write(\"</tr>\"          +
vbcrlf))");
    }
```

Horizontal with a Combobox.

```
    txtstream.OleFunction("WriteLine",OleVariant(\"Response.Write(\"<tr>\"     +
vbcrlf))");
    for(int b = 0; b < w; b++)
    {
        txtstream.OleFunction("WriteLine",OleVariant(\"Response.Write(\"<th
align='left' nowrap>" + Names[b] +"</th>\" + vbcrlf))");
    }

    for(int a = 0; a < v; a++)
```

```
        {
            txtstream.OleFunction("WriteLine",OleVariant(\"Response.Write(\"<tr>\"  +
vbcrlf))");
            for(int b = 0; b < w; b++)
            {
                txtstream.OleFunction("WriteLine",OleVariant(\"Response.Write(\"<td
style='font-family:Calibri,   Sans-Serif;font-size:   12px;color:navy;'   align='left'
nowrap='true'><select><option value  =  '"  +  Values[a][b]  +"'>"  +  Values[a][b]
+"</option></select></td>\" + vbcrlf))");
            }
            txtstream.OleFunction("WriteLine",OleVariant(\"Response.Write(\"</tr>\" +
vbcrlf))");
        }
```

Horizontal with a link.

```
        txtstream.OleFunction("WriteLine",OleVariant(\"Response.Write(\"<tr>\"     +
vbcrlf))");
        for(int b = 0; b < w; b++)
        {
            txtstream.OleFunction("WriteLine",OleVariant(\"Response.Write(\"<th
align='left' nowrap>" + Names[b] +"</th>\" + vbcrlf))");
        }


        for(int a = 0; a < v; a++)
        {
            txtstream.OleFunction("WriteLine",OleVariant(\"Response.Write(\"<tr>\"  +
vbcrlf))");
            for(int b = 0; b < w; b++)
            {

                txtstream.OleFunction("WriteLine",OleVariant(\"Response.Write(\"<td
style='font-family:Calibri,   Sans-Serif;font-size:   12px;color:navy;'   align='left'
nowrap='true'><a href='"  + Values[a][b] +"'>" + Values[a][b] +"</a></td>\"  +
vbcrlf))");
            }
            txtstream.OleFunction("WriteLine",OleVariant(\"Response.Write(\"</tr>\" +
vbcrlf))");
        }
```

Horizontal with a Listbox.

```
    txtstream.OleFunction("WriteLine",OleVariant(\"Response.Write(\"<tr>\"    +
vbcrlf))");
    for(int b = 0; b < w; b++)
    {
        txtstream.OleFunction("WriteLine",OleVariant(\"Response.Write(\"<th
align='left' nowrap>" + Names[b] +"</th>\" + vbcrlf))");
    }

    for(int a = 0; a < v; a++)
    {
        txtstream.OleFunction("WriteLine",OleVariant(\"Response.Write(\"<tr>\"   +
vbcrlf))");
        for(int b = 0; b < w; b++)
        {
            txtstream.OleFunction("WriteLine",OleVariant(\"Response.Write(\"<td
style='font-family:Calibri,   Sans-Serif;font-size:   12px;color:navy;'   align='left'
nowrap='true'><select  multiple><option  value  =  '" + Values[a][b] +"'>" +
Values[a][b] +"</option></select></td>\" + vbcrlf))");
        }
        txtstream.OleFunction("WriteLine",OleVariant(\"Response.Write(\"</tr>\" +
vbcrlf))");
    }
```

Horizontal with a textarea.

```
    txtstream.OleFunction("WriteLine",OleVariant(\"Response.Write(\"<tr>\"    +
vbcrlf))");
    for(int b = 0; b < w; b++)
    {
        txtstream.OleFunction("WriteLine",OleVariant(\"Response.Write(\"<th
align='left' nowrap>" + Names[b] +"</th>\" + vbcrlf))");
    }

    for(int a = 0; a < v; a++)
```

```
        {
        txtstream.OleFunction("WriteLine",OleVariant(\"Response.Write(\"<tr>\"   +
vbcrlf))");
            for(int b = 0; b < w; b++)
            {
            txtstream.OleFunction("WriteLine",OleVariant(\"Response.Write(\"<td
style='font-family:Calibri,    Sans-Serif;font-size:    12px;color:navy;'    align='left'
nowrap='true'><textarea>" + Values[a][b] +"</textarea></td>\" + vbcrlf))");
            }
        txtstream.OleFunction("WriteLine",OleVariant(\"Response.Write(\"</tr>\" +
vbcrlf))");
        }
```

Horizontal with a textbox.

```
        txtstream.OleFunction("WriteLine",OleVariant(\"Response.Write(\"<tr>\"      +
vbcrlf))");
        for(int b = 0; b < w; b++)
        {
        txtstream.OleFunction("WriteLine",OleVariant(\"Response.Write(\"<th
align='left' nowrap>" + Names[b] +"</th>\" + vbcrlf))");
        }


        for(int a = 0; a < v; a++)
        {
        txtstream.OleFunction("WriteLine",OleVariant(\"Response.Write(\"<tr>\"   +
vbcrlf))");
            for(int b = 0; b < w; b++)
            {
            txtstream.OleFunction("WriteLine",OleVariant(\"Response.Write(\"<td
style='font-family:Calibri,    Sans-Serif;font-size:    12px;color:navy;'    align='left'
nowrap='true'><input   type=text   value='"   +   Values[a][b]   +"'></input></td>\"   +
vbcrlf))");
            }
        txtstream.OleFunction("WriteLine",OleVariant(\"Response.Write(\"</tr>\" +
vbcrlf))");
        }
```

Vertical with no additional tags.

```
for(int b = 0; b < w; b++)
{
```

txtstream.OleFunction("WriteLine",OleVariant(\"Response.Write(\"<tr><th align='left' nowrap>" + Names[b] +"</th>\" + vbcrlf))");

```
    for(int a = 0; a < v; a++)
    {
```

txtstream.OleFunction("WriteLine",OleVariant(\"Response.Write(\"<td style='font-family:Calibri, Sans-Serif;font-size: 12px;color:navy;' align='left' nowrap='nowrap'>" + Values[a][b] +"</td>\" + vbcrlf))");

```
    }
```

txtstream.OleFunction("WriteLine",OleVariant(\"Response.Write(\"</tr>\"   + vbcrlf))");

```
}
```

Vertical with a Combobox.

```
for(int b = 0; b < w; b++)
{
```

txtstream.OleFunction("WriteLine",OleVariant(\"Response.Write(\"<tr><th align='left' nowrap>" + Names[b] +"</th>\" + vbcrlf))");

```
    for(int a = 0; a < v; a++)
    {
```

txtstream.OleFunction("WriteLine",OleVariant(\"Response.Write(\"<td style='font-family:Calibri, Sans-Serif;font-size: 12px;color:navy;' align='left' nowrap='true'><select><option value = "'" + Values[a][b] +"'">" + Values[a][b] +"</option></select></td>\" + vbcrlf))");

```
    }
```

txtstream.OleFunction("WriteLine",OleVariant(\"Response.Write(\"</tr>\"   + vbcrlf))");

```
}
```

Vertical with a link.

```
for(int b = 0; b < w; b++)
{

txtstream.OleFunction("WriteLine",OleVariant(\"Response.Write(\"<tr><th
align='left' nowrap>" + Names[b] +"</th>\" + vbcrlf))");
    for(int a = 0; a < v; a++)
    {
        txtstream.OleFunction("WriteLine",OleVariant(\"Response.Write(\"<td
style='font-family:Calibri,    Sans-Serif;font-size:    12px;color:navy;'    align='left'
nowrap='true'><a href='" + Values[a][b] +"'>" + Values[a][b] +"</a></td>\" +
vbcrlf))");
    }

txtstream.OleFunction("WriteLine",OleVariant(\"Response.Write(\"</tr>\"        +
vbcrlf))");
}
```

Vertical with a Listbox.

```
for(int b = 0; b < w; b++)
{

txtstream.OleFunction("WriteLine",OleVariant(\"Response.Write(\"<tr><th
align='left' nowrap>" + Names[b] +"</th>\" + vbcrlf))");
    for(int a = 0; a < v; a++)
    {
        txtstream.OleFunction("WriteLine",OleVariant(\"Response.Write(\"<td
style='font-family:Calibri,    Sans-Serif;font-size:    12px;color:navy;'    align='left'
nowrap='true'><select multiple><option value = "'" + Values[a][b] +"'">" +
Values[a][b] +"</option></select></td>\" + vbcrlf))");
    }
        txtstream.OleFunction("WriteLine",OleVariant(\"Response.Write(\"</tr>\" +
vbcrlf))");
}
```

Vertical with a textarea.

```
for(int b = 0; b < w; b++)
{

txtstream.OleFunction("WriteLine",OleVariant(\"Response.Write(\"<tr><th
align='left' nowrap>" + Names[b] +"</th>\" + vbcrlf))");
    for(int a = 0; a < v; a++)
    {
        txtstream.OleFunction("WriteLine",OleVariant(\"Response.Write(\"<td
style='font-family:Calibri,    Sans-Serif;font-size:    12px;color:navy;'    align='left'
nowrap='true'><textarea>" + Values[a][b] +"</textarea></td>\" + vbcrlf))");
    }

txtstream.OleFunction("WriteLine",OleVariant(\"Response.Write(\"</tr>\"        +
vbcrlf))");
}
```

Vertical with a textbox.

```
for(int b = 0; b < w; b++)
{

txtstream.OleFunction("WriteLine",OleVariant(\"Response.Write(\"<tr><th
align='left' nowrap>" + Names[b] +"</th>\" + vbcrlf))");
    for(int a = 0; a < v; a++)
    {
        txtstream.OleFunction("WriteLine",OleVariant(\"Response.Write(\"<td
style='font-family:Calibri,    Sans-Serif;font-size:    12px;color:navy;'    align='left'
nowrap='true'><input type=text value="'" + Values[a][b] +"'"></input></td>\" +
vbcrlf))");
    }
        txtstream.OleFunction("WriteLine",OleVariant(\"Response.Write(\"</tr>\" +
vbcrlf))");
}
```

End Code

```
txtstream.OleFunction("WriteLine",OleVariant(\"</table>\"))");
txtstream.OleFunction("WriteLine",OleVariant(\"</body>\"))");
txtstream.OleFunction("WriteLine",OleVariant(\"</html>\"))");
txtstream.close();
```

```
Variant ws = Variant::CreateObject("WScript.Shell");
String CurrentDirectory = ws.OlePropertyGet("CurrentDirectory");
CurrentDirectory = CurrentDirectory + "\\Win32_Process.hta";
Variant fso = Variant::CreateObject("Scripting.FileSystemObject");
Variant        txtstream        =        fso.OleFunction("OpenTextFile",
OleVariant(CurrentDirectory), OleVariant(2), OleVariant(true), OleVariant(-2));

    txtstream.OleFunction("WriteLine",OleVariant(\"<html
xmlns='http://www.w3.org/1999/xhtml'>\"))");
    txtstream.OleFunction("WriteLine",OleVariant(\"<head>\"))");
    txtstream.OleFunction("WriteLine",OleVariant(\"<HTA:APPLICATION ");
    txtstream.OleFunction("WriteLine",OleVariant(\"ID = ""Process"" ");
    txtstream.OleFunction("WriteLine",OleVariant(\"APPLICATIONNAME        =
""Process"" ");
    txtstream.OleFunction("WriteLine",OleVariant(\"SCROLL = ""yes"" ");
    txtstream.OleFunction("WriteLine",OleVariant(\"SINGLEINSTANCE  =  ""yes""
");
    txtstream.OleFunction("WriteLine",OleVariant(\"WINDOWSTATE            =
""maximize"" >\"))");
    txtstream.OleFunction("WriteLine",OleVariant(\"</head>\"))");
    txtstream.OleFunction("WriteLine",OleVariant(\"<body>\"))");
    txtstream.OleFunction("WriteLine",OleVariant(\"<table            border='1'
Cellspacing='3' cellpadding = '3'>\"))");
```

Horizontal with no additional tags.

```
txtstream.OleFunction("WriteLine",OleVariant("<tr>"));
for(int b = 0; b < w; b++)
{
    txtstream.OleFunction("WriteLine",OleVariant("<th align='left' nowrap>" +
Names[b] +"</th>"));
}
txtstream.OleFunction("WriteLine",OleVariant("</tr>"));
for(int a = 0; a < v; a++)
{
    txtstream.OleFunction("WriteLine",OleVariant("<tr>"));
    for(int b = 0; b < w; b++)
    {
        txtstream.OleFunction("WriteLine",OleVariant("<td          style='font-
family:Calibri,      Sans-Serif;font-size:      12px;color:navy;'      align='left'
nowrap='nowrap'>" + Values[a][b] +"</td>"));
    }
    txtstream.OleFunction("WriteLine",OleVariant("</tr>"));
}
```

Horizontal with a Combobox.

```
txtstream.OleFunction("WriteLine",OleVariant("<tr>"));
for(int b = 0; b < w; b++)
{
    txtstream.OleFunction("WriteLine",OleVariant("<th align='left' nowrap>" +
Names[b] +"</th>"));
}

for(int a = 0; a < v; a++)
{
    txtstream.OleFunction("WriteLine",OleVariant("<tr>"));
    for(int b = 0; b < w; b++)
    {
        txtstream.OleFunction("WriteLine",OleVariant("<td          style='font-
family:Calibri,      Sans-Serif;font-size:      12px;color:navy;'      align='left'
nowrap='true'><select><option value = '" + Values[a][b] +"'>" + Values[a][b]
+"</option></select></td>"));
    }
    txtstream.OleFunction("WriteLine",OleVariant("</tr>"));
```

```
        }
```

Horizontal with a link.

```
        txtstream.OleFunction("WriteLine",OleVariant("<tr>"));
        for(int b = 0; b < w; b++)
        {
            txtstream.OleFunction("WriteLine",OleVariant("<th align='left' nowrap>" +
Names[b] +"</th>"));
        }


        for(int a = 0; a < v; a++)
        {
            txtstream.OleFunction("WriteLine",OleVariant("<tr>"));
            for(int b = 0; b < w; b++)
            {

                txtstream.OleFunction("WriteLine",OleVariant("<td          style='font-
family:Calibri, Sans-Serif;font-size: 12px;color:navy;' align='left' nowrap='true'><a
href='" + Values[a][b] +"'>" + Values[a][b] +"</a></td>"));
            }
            txtstream.OleFunction("WriteLine",OleVariant("</tr>"));
        }
```

Horizontal with a Listbox.

```
        txtstream.OleFunction("WriteLine",OleVariant("<tr>"));
        for(int b = 0; b < w; b++)
        {
            txtstream.OleFunction("WriteLine",OleVariant("<th align='left' nowrap>" +
Names[b] +"</th>"));
        }

        for(int a = 0; a < v; a++)
        {
            txtstream.OleFunction("WriteLine",OleVariant("<tr>"));
            for(int b = 0; b < w; b++)
            {
```

```
        txtstream.OleFunction("WriteLine",OleVariant("<td                style='font-
family:Calibri,         Sans-Serif;font-size:         12px;color:navy;'        align='left'
nowrap='true'><select   multiple><option   value   =   '"   +   Values[a][b]   +"'>"   +
Values[a][b] +"</option></select></td>"));
        }
        txtstream.OleFunction("WriteLine",OleVariant("</tr>"));
    }
```

Horizontal with a textarea.

```
    txtstream.OleFunction("WriteLine",OleVariant("<tr>"));
    for(int b = 0; b < w; b++)
    {
        txtstream.OleFunction("WriteLine",OleVariant("<th align='left' nowrap>" +
Names[b] +"</th>"));
    }

    for(int a = 0; a < v; a++)
    {
        txtstream.OleFunction("WriteLine",OleVariant("<tr>"));
        for(int b = 0; b < w; b++)
        {
            txtstream.OleFunction("WriteLine",OleVariant("<td                style='font-
family:Calibri,         Sans-Serif;font-size:         12px;color:navy;'         align='left'
nowrap='true'><textarea>" + Values[a][b] +"</textarea></td>"));
        }
        txtstream.OleFunction("WriteLine",OleVariant("</tr>"));
    }
```

Horizontal with a textbox.

```
    txtstream.OleFunction("WriteLine",OleVariant("<tr>"));
    for(int b = 0; b < w; b++)
    {
        txtstream.OleFunction("WriteLine",OleVariant("<th align='left' nowrap>" +
Names[b] +"</th>"));
    }
```

```
for(int a = 0; a < v; a++)
{
    txtstream.OleFunction("WriteLine",OleVariant("<tr>"));
    for(int b = 0; b < w; b++)
    {
        txtstream.OleFunction("WriteLine",OleVariant("<td          style='font-
family:Calibri,       Sans-Serif;font-size:      12px;color:navy;'      align='left'
nowrap='true'><input type=text value='" + Values[a][b] +"'></input></td>"));
    }
    txtstream.OleFunction("WriteLine",OleVariant("</tr>"));
}
```

Vertical with no additional tags.

```
for(int b = 0; b < w; b++)
{
    txtstream.OleFunction("WriteLine",OleVariant("<tr><th         align='left'
nowrap>" + Names[b] +"</th>"));
    for(int a = 0; a < v; a++)
    {
        txtstream.OleFunction("WriteLine",OleVariant("<td          style='font-
family:Calibri,       Sans-Serif;font-size:      12px;color:navy;'      align='left'
nowrap='nowrap'>" + Values[a][b] +"</td>"));
    }
    txtstream.OleFunction("WriteLine",OleVariant("</tr>"));
}
```

Vertical with a Combobox.

```
for(int b = 0; b < w; b++)
{
    txtstream.OleFunction("WriteLine",OleVariant("<tr><th         align='left'
nowrap>" + Names[b] +"</th>"));
    for(int a = 0; a < v; a++)
    {
```

```
        txtstream.OleFunction("WriteLine",OleVariant("<td          style='font-
family:Calibri,     Sans-Serif;font-size:        12px;color:navy;'     align='left'
nowrap='true'><select><option value = """ + Values[a][b] +""">" + Values[a][b]
+"</option></select></td>"));
        }
        txtstream.OleFunction("WriteLine",OleVariant("</tr>"));
    }
```

Vertical with a link.

```
    for(int b = 0; b < w; b++)
    {
        txtstream.OleFunction("WriteLine",OleVariant("<tr><th          align='left'
nowrap>" + Names[b] +"</th>"));
        for(int a = 0; a < v; a++)
        {
        txtstream.OleFunction("WriteLine",OleVariant("<td               style='font-
family:Calibri, Sans-Serif;font-size: 12px;color:navy;' align='left' nowrap='true'><a
href='" + Values[a][b] +"'>" + Values[a][b] +"</a></td>"));
        }
        txtstream.OleFunction("WriteLine",OleVariant("</tr>"));
    }
```

Vertical with a Listbox.

```
    for(int b = 0; b < w; b++)
    {
        txtstream.OleFunction("WriteLine",OleVariant("<tr><th          align='left'
nowrap>" + Names[b] +"</th>"));
        for(int a = 0; a < v; a++)
        {
        txtstream.OleFunction("WriteLine",OleVariant("<td               style='font-
family:Calibri,     Sans-Serif;font-size:        12px;color:navy;'     align='left'
nowrap='true'><select  multiple><option value = """  + Values[a][b]  +""">"  +
Values[a][b] +"</option></select></td>"));
        }
        txtstream.OleFunction("WriteLine",OleVariant("</tr>"));
    }
```

Vertical with a textarea.

```
for(int b = 0; b < w; b++)
{
    txtstream.OleFunction("WriteLine",OleVariant("<tr><th          align='left'
nowrap>" + Names[b] +"</th>"));
    for(int a = 0; a < v; a++)
    {
        txtstream.OleFunction("WriteLine",OleVariant("<td                 style='font-
family:Calibri,      Sans-Serif;font-size:      12px;color:navy;'      align='left'
nowrap='true'><textarea>" + Values[a][b] +"</textarea></td>"));
    }
        txtstream.OleFunction("WriteLine",OleVariant("</tr>"));
}
```

Vertical with a textbox.

```
for(int b = 0; b < w; b++)
{
    txtstream.OleFunction("WriteLine",OleVariant("<tr><th          align='left'
nowrap>" + Names[b] +"</th>"));
    for(int a = 0; a < v; a++)
    {
        txtstream.OleFunction("WriteLine",OleVariant("<td                 style='font-
family:Calibri,      Sans-Serif;font-size:      12px;color:navy;'      align='left'
nowrap='true'><input type=text value="'" + Values[a][b] +"'"></input></td>"));
    }
        txtstream.OleFunction("WriteLine",OleVariant("</tr>"));
}
```

End Code

```
txtstream.OleFunction("WriteLine",OleVariant(\"</table>\"))");
txtstream.OleFunction("WriteLine",OleVariant(\"</body>\"))");
txtstream.OleFunction("WriteLine",OleVariant(\"</html>\"))");
txtstream.close();
```

HTML Reports

Begin Code

```
Variant ws = Variant::CreateObject("WScript.Shell");
String CurrentDirectory = ws.OlePropertyGet("CurrentDirectory");
CurrentDirectory = CurrentDirectory + "\\Win32_Process.html";
Variant fso = Variant::CreateObject("Scripting.FileSystemObject");
Variant          txtstream          =          fso.OleFunction("OpenTextFile",
OleVariant(CurrentDirectory), OleVariant(2), OleVariant(true), OleVariant(-2));
    txtstream.OleFunction("WriteLine",OleVariant(\"<html
xmlns='http://www.w3.org/1999/xhtml'>\"))");
    txtstream.OleFunction("WriteLine",OleVariant(\"<head>\"))");
    txtstream.OleFunction("WriteLine",OleVariant(\"<title>Win32_Process</title>
\"))");
    txtstream.OleFunction("WriteLine",OleVariant(\"</head>\"))");
    txtstream.OleFunction("WriteLine",OleVariant(\"<body>\"))");
    txtstream.OleFunction("WriteLine",OleVariant(\"<table              border='0'
Cellspacing='3' cellpadding = '3'>\"))");
```

Horizontal with no additional tags.

```
    txtstream.OleFunction("WriteLine",OleVariant("<tr>"));
    for(int b = 0; b < w; b++)
    {
```

```
        txtstream.OleFunction("WriteLine",OleVariant("<th align='left' nowrap>" +
Names[b] +"</th>"));
    }
    txtstream.OleFunction("WriteLine",OleVariant("</tr>"));
    for(int a = 0; a < v; a++)
    {
        txtstream.OleFunction("WriteLine",OleVariant("<tr>"));
        for(int b = 0; b < w; b++)
        {
            txtstream.OleFunction("WriteLine",OleVariant("<td          style='font-
family:Calibri,     Sans-Serif;font-size:    12px;color:navy;'    align='left'
nowrap='nowrap'>" + Values[a][b] +"</td>"));
        }
        txtstream.OleFunction("WriteLine",OleVariant("</tr>"));
    }
```

Horizontal with a Combobox.

```
    txtstream.OleFunction("WriteLine",OleVariant("<tr>"));
    for(int b = 0; b < w; b++)
    {
        txtstream.OleFunction("WriteLine",OleVariant("<th align='left' nowrap>" +
Names[b] +"</th>"));
    }

    for(int a = 0; a < v; a++)
    {
        txtstream.OleFunction("WriteLine",OleVariant("<tr>"));
        for(int b = 0; b < w; b++)
        {
            txtstream.OleFunction("WriteLine",OleVariant("<td          style='font-
family:Calibri,     Sans-Serif;font-size:    12px;color:navy;'    align='left'
nowrap='true'><select><option value = '" + Values[a][b] +"'>" + Values[a][b]
+"</option></select></td>"));
        }
        txtstream.OleFunction("WriteLine",OleVariant("</tr>"));
    }
```

Horizontal with a link.

```
txtstream.OleFunction("WriteLine",OleVariant("<tr>"));
for(int b = 0; b < w; b++)
{
    txtstream.OleFunction("WriteLine",OleVariant("<th align='left' nowrap>" +
Names[b] +"</th>"));
}


for(int a = 0; a < v; a++)
{
    txtstream.OleFunction("WriteLine",OleVariant("<tr>"));
    for(int b = 0; b < w; b++)
    {

        txtstream.OleFunction("WriteLine",OleVariant("<td          style='font-
family:Calibri, Sans-Serif;font-size: 12px;color:navy;' align='left' nowrap='true'><a
href='" + Values[a][b] +"'>" + Values[a][b] +"</a></td>"));
    }
    txtstream.OleFunction("WriteLine",OleVariant("</tr>"));
}
```

Horizontal with a Listbox.

```
txtstream.OleFunction("WriteLine",OleVariant("<tr>"));
for(int b = 0; b < w; b++)
{
    txtstream.OleFunction("WriteLine",OleVariant("<th align='left' nowrap>" +
Names[b] +"</th>"));
}

for(int a = 0; a < v; a++)
{
    txtstream.OleFunction("WriteLine",OleVariant("<tr>"));
    for(int b = 0; b < w; b++)
    {
        txtstream.OleFunction("WriteLine",OleVariant("<td          style='font-
family:Calibri,     Sans-Serif;font-size:      12px;color:navy;'      align='left'
```

```
nowrap='true'><select multiple><option value = '" + Values[a][b] +"'>" +
Values[a][b] +"</option></select></td>"));
        }
        txtstream.OleFunction("WriteLine",OleVariant("</tr>"));
    }
```

Horizontal with a textarea.

```
        txtstream.OleFunction("WriteLine",OleVariant("<tr>"));
        for(int b = 0; b < w; b++)
        {
            txtstream.OleFunction("WriteLine",OleVariant("<th align='left' nowrap>" +
Names[b] +"</th>"));
        }


        for(int a = 0; a < v; a++)
        {
            txtstream.OleFunction("WriteLine",OleVariant("<tr>"));
            for(int b = 0; b < w; b++)
            {
                txtstream.OleFunction("WriteLine",OleVariant("<td          style='font-
family:Calibri,      Sans-Serif;font-size:      12px;color:navy;'    align='left'
nowrap='true'><textarea>" + Values[a][b] +"</textarea></td>"));
            }
            txtstream.OleFunction("WriteLine",OleVariant("</tr>"));
        }
```

Horizontal with a textbox.

```
        txtstream.OleFunction("WriteLine",OleVariant("<tr>"));
        for(int b = 0; b < w; b++)
        {
            txtstream.OleFunction("WriteLine",OleVariant("<th align='left' nowrap>" +
Names[b] +"</th>"));
        }


        for(int a = 0; a < v; a++)
```

```
        {
            txtstream.OleFunction("WriteLine",OleVariant("<tr>"));
            for(int b = 0; b < w; b++)
            {
                txtstream.OleFunction("WriteLine",OleVariant("<td          style='font-
family:Calibri,     Sans-Serif;font-size:     12px;color:navy;'     align='left'
nowrap='true'><input type=text value='" + Values[a][b] +"'></input></td>"));
            }
            txtstream.OleFunction("WriteLine",OleVariant("</tr>"));
        }
```

Vertical with no additional tags.

```
    for(int b = 0; b < w; b++)
    {
        txtstream.OleFunction("WriteLine",OleVariant("<tr><th        align='left'
nowrap>" + Names[b] +"</th>"));
        for(int a = 0; a < v; a++)
        {
            txtstream.OleFunction("WriteLine",OleVariant("<td          style='font-
family:Calibri,     Sans-Serif;font-size:     12px;color:navy;'     align='left'
nowrap='nowrap'>" + Values[a][b] +"</td>"));
        }
        txtstream.OleFunction("WriteLine",OleVariant("</tr>"));
    }
```

Vertical with a Combobox.

```
    for(int b = 0; b < w; b++)
    {
        txtstream.OleFunction("WriteLine",OleVariant("<tr><th        align='left'
nowrap>" + Names[b] +"</th>"));
        for(int a = 0; a < v; a++)
        {
            txtstream.OleFunction("WriteLine",OleVariant("<td          style='font-
family:Calibri,     Sans-Serif;font-size:     12px;color:navy;'     align='left'
```

```
nowrap='true'><select><option value = """ + Values[a][b] +""">" + Values[a][b]
+"</option></select></td>“));
        }
            txtstream.OleFunction(“WriteLine”,OleVariant(“</tr>“));
    }
```

Vertical with a link.

```
    for(int b = 0; b < w; b++)
    {
        txtstream.OleFunction(“WriteLine”,OleVariant(“<tr><th        align='left'
nowrap>" + Names[b] +"</th>“));
        for(int a = 0; a < v; a++)
        {
            txtstream.OleFunction(“WriteLine”,OleVariant(“<td            style='font-
family:Calibri, Sans-Serif;font-size: 12px;color:navy;' align='left' nowrap='true'><a
href='" + Values[a][b] +"'>" + Values[a][b] +"</a></td>“));
        }
            txtstream.OleFunction(“WriteLine”,OleVariant(“</tr>“));
    }
```

Vertical with a Listbox.

```
    for(int b = 0; b < w; b++)
    {
        txtstream.OleFunction(“WriteLine”,OleVariant(“<tr><th        align='left'
nowrap>" + Names[b] +"</th>“));
        for(int a = 0; a < v; a++)
        {
            txtstream.OleFunction(“WriteLine”,OleVariant(“<td            style='font-
family:Calibri,        Sans-Serif;font-size:        12px;color:navy;'        align='left'
nowrap='true'><select multiple><option value = """ + Values[a][b] +""">" +
Values[a][b] +"</option></select></td>“));
        }
        txtstream.OleFunction(“WriteLine”,OleVariant(“</tr>“));
    }
```
Vertical with a textarea.

```
    for(int b = 0; b < w; b++)
```

```
        {
                txtstream.OleFunction("WriteLine",OleVariant("<tr><th        align='left'
nowrap>" + Names[b] +"</th>"));
            for(int a = 0; a < v; a++)
            {
                txtstream.OleFunction("WriteLine",OleVariant("<td            style='font-
family:Calibri,        Sans-Serif;font-size:        12px;color:navy;'        align='left'
nowrap='true'><textarea>" + Values[a][b] +"</textarea></td>"));
            }
                txtstream.OleFunction("WriteLine",OleVariant("</tr>"));
        }
```

Vertical with a textbox.

```
        for(int b = 0; b < w; b++)
        {
                txtstream.OleFunction("WriteLine",OleVariant("<tr><th        align='left'
nowrap>" + Names[b] +"</th>"));
            for(int a = 0; a < v; a++)
            {
                txtstream.OleFunction("WriteLine",OleVariant("<td            style='font-
family:Calibri,        Sans-Serif;font-size:        12px;color:navy;'        align='left'
nowrap='true'><input type=text value="'" + Values[a][b] +"'"></input></td>"));
            }
            txtstream.OleFunction("WriteLine",OleVariant("</tr>"));
        }
```

End Code

```
        txtstream.OleFunction("WriteLine",OleVariant(\"</table>\"))");
        txtstream.OleFunction("WriteLine",OleVariant(\"</body>\"))");
        txtstream.OleFunction("WriteLine",OleVariant(\"</html>\"))");
        txtstream.close();
```

Begin Code

```
    Variant ws = Variant::CreateObject("WScript.Shell");
    String CurrentDirectory = ws.OlePropertyGet("CurrentDirectory");
    CurrentDirectory = CurrentDirectory + "\\Win32_Process.html";
    Variant fso = Variant::CreateObject("Scripting.FileSystemObject");
    Variant       txtstream       =       fso.OleFunction("OpenTextFile",
OleVariant(CurrentDirectory), OleVariant(2), OleVariant(true), OleVariant(-2));
    txtstream.OleFunction("WriteLine",OleVariant(\"<html
xmlns='http://www.w3.org/1999/xhtml'>\"))");
    txtstream.OleFunction("WriteLine",OleVariant(\"<head>\"))");
    txtstream.OleFunction("WriteLine",OleVariant(\"<title>Win32_Process</title>
\"))");
    txtstream.OleFunction("WriteLine",OleVariant(\"</head>\"))");
    txtstream.OleFunction("WriteLine",OleVariant(\"<body>\"))");
    txtstream.OleFunction("WriteLine",OleVariant(\"<table              border='1'
Cellspacing='3' cellpadding = '3'>\"))");
```

Horizontal with no additional tags.

Horizontal with no additional tags.

```
    txtstream.OleFunction("WriteLine",OleVariant("<tr>"));
    for(int b = 0; b < w; b++)
    {
```

```
        txtstream.OleFunction("WriteLine",OleVariant("<th align='left' nowrap>" +
Names[b] +"</th>"));
    }
    txtstream.OleFunction("WriteLine",OleVariant("</tr>"));
    for(int a = 0; a < v; a++)
    {
        txtstream.OleFunction("WriteLine",OleVariant("<tr>"));
        for(int b = 0; b < w; b++)
        {
            txtstream.OleFunction("WriteLine",OleVariant("<td          style='font-
family:Calibri,      Sans-Serif;font-size:        12px;color:navy;'       align='left'
nowrap='nowrap'>" + Values[a][b] +"</td>"));
        }
        txtstream.OleFunction("WriteLine",OleVariant("</tr>"));
    }
```

Horizontal with a Combobox.

```
    txtstream.OleFunction("WriteLine",OleVariant("<tr>"));
    for(int b = 0; b < w; b++)
    {
        txtstream.OleFunction("WriteLine",OleVariant("<th align='left' nowrap>" +
Names[b] +"</th>"));
    }

    for(int a = 0; a < v; a++)
    {
        txtstream.OleFunction("WriteLine",OleVariant("<tr>"));
        for(int b = 0; b < w; b++)
        {
            txtstream.OleFunction("WriteLine",OleVariant("<td          style='font-
family:Calibri,      Sans-Serif;font-size:        12px;color:navy;'       align='left'
nowrap='true'><select><option value = '" + Values[a][b] +"'>" + Values[a][b]
+"</option></select></td>"));
        }
        txtstream.OleFunction("WriteLine",OleVariant("</tr>"));
    }
```

Horizontal with a link.

```
txtstream.OleFunction("WriteLine",OleVariant("<tr>"));
for(int b = 0; b < w; b++)
{
    txtstream.OleFunction("WriteLine",OleVariant("<th align='left' nowrap>" +
Names[b] +"</th>"));
}


for(int a = 0; a < v; a++)
{
    txtstream.OleFunction("WriteLine",OleVariant("<tr>"));
    for(int b = 0; b < w; b++)
    {

        txtstream.OleFunction("WriteLine",OleVariant("<td          style='font-
family:Calibri, Sans-Serif;font-size: 12px;color:navy;' align='left' nowrap='true'><a
href='" + Values[a][b] +"'>" + Values[a][b] +"</a></td>"));
    }
    txtstream.OleFunction("WriteLine",OleVariant("</tr>"));
}
```

Horizontal with a Listbox.

```
txtstream.OleFunction("WriteLine",OleVariant("<tr>"));
for(int b = 0; b < w; b++)
{
    txtstream.OleFunction("WriteLine",OleVariant("<th align='left' nowrap>" +
Names[b] +"</th>"));
}

for(int a = 0; a < v; a++)
{
    txtstream.OleFunction("WriteLine",OleVariant("<tr>"));
    for(int b = 0; b < w; b++)
    {
        txtstream.OleFunction("WriteLine",OleVariant("<td          style='font-
family:Calibri,     Sans-Serif;font-size:     12px;color:navy;'     align='left'
```

```
nowrap='true'><select multiple><option value = '" + Values[a][b] +"'>" +
Values[a][b] +"</option></select></td>"));
        }
        txtstream.OleFunction("WriteLine",OleVariant("</tr>"));
    }
```

Horizontal with a textarea.

```
    txtstream.OleFunction("WriteLine",OleVariant("<tr>"));
    for(int b = 0; b < w; b++)
    {
        txtstream.OleFunction("WriteLine",OleVariant("<th align='left' nowrap>" +
Names[b] +"</th>"));
    }


    for(int a = 0; a < v; a++)
    {
        txtstream.OleFunction("WriteLine",OleVariant("<tr>"));
        for(int b = 0; b < w; b++)
        {
            txtstream.OleFunction("WriteLine",OleVariant("<td                style='font-
family:Calibri,       Sans-Serif;font-size:       12px;color:navy;'      align='left'
nowrap='true'><textarea>" + Values[a][b] +"</textarea></td>"));
        }
        txtstream.OleFunction("WriteLine",OleVariant("</tr>"));
    }
```

Horizontal with a textbox.

```
    txtstream.OleFunction("WriteLine",OleVariant("<tr>"));
    for(int b = 0; b < w; b++)
    {
        txtstream.OleFunction("WriteLine",OleVariant("<th align='left' nowrap>" +
Names[b] +"</th>"));
    }


    for(int a = 0; a < v; a++)
```

```
    {
        txtstream.OleFunction("WriteLine",OleVariant("<tr>"));
        for(int b = 0; b < w; b++)
        {
            txtstream.OleFunction("WriteLine",OleVariant("<td            style='font-
family:Calibri,      Sans-Serif;font-size:      12px;color:navy;'      align='left'
nowrap='true'><input type=text value='" + Values[a][b] +"'></input></td>"));
        }
        txtstream.OleFunction("WriteLine",OleVariant("</tr>"));
    }
```

Vertical with no additional tags.

```
    for(int b = 0; b < w; b++)
    {
        txtstream.OleFunction("WriteLine",OleVariant("<tr><th        align='left'
nowrap>" + Names[b] +"</th>"));
        for(int a = 0; a < v; a++)
        {
            txtstream.OleFunction("WriteLine",OleVariant("<td            style='font-
family:Calibri,      Sans-Serif;font-size:      12px;color:navy;'      align='left'
nowrap='nowrap'>" + Values[a][b] +"</td>"));
        }
        txtstream.OleFunction("WriteLine",OleVariant("</tr>"));
    }
```

Vertical with a Combobox.

```
    for(int b = 0; b < w; b++)
    {
        txtstream.OleFunction("WriteLine",OleVariant("<tr><th        align='left'
nowrap>" + Names[b] +"</th>"));
        for(int a = 0; a < v; a++)
        {
            txtstream.OleFunction("WriteLine",OleVariant("<td            style='font-
family:Calibri,      Sans-Serif;font-size:      12px;color:navy;'      align='left'
```

```
nowrap='true'><select><option value = """ + Values[a][b] +""">" + Values[a][b]
+"</option></select></td>"));
            }
        txtstream.OleFunction("WriteLine",OleVariant("</tr>"));
    }
```

Vertical with a link.

```
    for(int b = 0; b < w; b++)
    {
        txtstream.OleFunction("WriteLine",OleVariant("<tr><th        align='left'
nowrap>" + Names[b] +"</th>"));
        for(int a = 0; a < v; a++)
        {
            txtstream.OleFunction("WriteLine",OleVariant("<td            style='font-
family:Calibri, Sans-Serif;font-size: 12px;color:navy;' align='left' nowrap='true'><a
href='" + Values[a][b] +"'>" + Values[a][b] +"</a></td>"));
        }
        txtstream.OleFunction("WriteLine",OleVariant("</tr>"));
    }
```

Vertical with a Listbox.

```
    for(int b = 0; b < w; b++)
    {
        txtstream.OleFunction("WriteLine",OleVariant("<tr><th        align='left'
nowrap>" + Names[b] +"</th>"));
        for(int a = 0; a < v; a++)
        {
            txtstream.OleFunction("WriteLine",OleVariant("<td            style='font-
family:Calibri,      Sans-Serif;font-size:      12px;color:navy;'      align='left'
nowrap='true'><select  multiple><option value = """  + Values[a][b] +""">"  +
Values[a][b] +"</option></select></td>"));
        }
        txtstream.OleFunction("WriteLine",OleVariant("</tr>"));
    }
```

Vertical with a textarea.

```
    for(int b = 0; b < w; b++)
```

```
    {
        txtstream.OleFunction("WriteLine",OleVariant("<tr><th          align='left'
nowrap>" + Names[b] +"</th>"));
        for(int a = 0; a < v; a++)
        {
            txtstream.OleFunction("WriteLine",OleVariant("<td            style='font-
family:Calibri,      Sans-Serif;font-size:        12px;color:navy;'      align='left'
nowrap='true'><textarea>" + Values[a][b] +"</textarea></td>"));
        }
            txtstream.OleFunction("WriteLine",OleVariant("</tr>"));
    }
```

Vertical with a textbox.

```
    for(int b = 0; b < w; b++)
    {
        txtstream.OleFunction("WriteLine",OleVariant("<tr><th          align='left'
nowrap>" + Names[b] +"</th>"));
        for(int a = 0; a < v; a++)
        {
            txtstream.OleFunction("WriteLine",OleVariant("<td            style='font-
family:Calibri,      Sans-Serif;font-size:        12px;color:navy;'      align='left'
nowrap='true'><input type=text value="""" + Values[a][b] +""""></input></td>"));
        }
        txtstream.OleFunction("WriteLine",OleVariant("</tr>"));
    }
```

End Code

```
    txtstream.OleFunction("WriteLine",OleVariant(\"</table>\")")");
    txtstream.OleFunction("WriteLine",OleVariant(\"</body>\")")");
    txtstream.OleFunction("WriteLine",OleVariant(\"</html>\")")");
    txtstream.close();
```

The Empty Template

```cpp
//----------------------------------------------------------------
#include <vcl.h>
#pragma hdrstop
#include "ComObj.hpp"
#include "Unit1.h"
#include <iostream>
#include <utility>
using namespace std;
//----------------------------------------------------------------
//----------
#pragma package(smart_init)
#pragma resource "*.dfm"
TForm1 *Form1;
//----------------------------------------------------------------
//----------
__fastcall TForm1::TForm1(TComponent* Owner)
        : TForm(Owner)
{
}
//----------------------------------------------------------------

String* Names;
String** Values;

int v = 0;
int w = 0;

void WriteTheCode()
{


}
```

```
String GetValue(String N, Variant obj)
{
    int pos = 0;
    String Tempstr = obj.OleFunction("GetObjectText_");
    N = N + " = ";
    String Ne = N;
    pos = AnsiPos(Ne, Tempstr);
    if(pos > 0)
    {
        pos = pos + Ne.Length();
        int l = Tempstr.Length();
        Tempstr = Tempstr.SubString(pos, l);
        pos = AnsiPos(";", Tempstr);
        Tempstr = Tempstr.SubString(2, pos -3);
        return Tempstr;
    }
    else
    {
        return "";
    }
}
void BuildTheArray(Variant es)
{
        LPUNKNOWN punkEnum;
        IEnumVARIANT * propEnum=NULL;
        VARIANT tprop;
        VariantInit(&tprop);
        int nIndex;
        unsigned long c;

        while(v < 4)
        {
                Variant o = es.OleFunction("NextEvent", OleVariant(-1));
                Variant props = o.OlePropertyGet("Properties_");
                Variant Item = props.OleFunction("Item",
OleVariant("TargetInstance"));
                Variant obj = Item.OlePropertyGet("Value");
                Variant propSet = obj.OlePropertyGet("Properties_");
                w = propSet.OlePropertyGet("Count");
                        if(v == 0)
                {
                        int x = 0;
                        Names = new String[w];
                        Values = new String*[4];
                        for(int i = 0; i < 4; i++)
                        {
                                Values[i] = new String[w];
                        }
                        punkEnum = propSet.OlePropertyGet("_NewEnum");
```

```cpp
                        punkEnum->QueryInterface(IID_IEnumVARIANT,
(LPVOID far*)&propEnum);
                        propEnum->AddRef();
                        punkEnum->Release();
                        while(propEnum->Next(1, &tprop, &c) == S_OK)
                        {
                                Variant prop = Variant(tprop);
                                String Name = prop.OlePropertyGet("Name");
                                Names[x] = Name;
                                String Value = GetValue(Name, obj);
                                Values[v][x] = Value;
                                x = x + 1;
                        }
                        x = 0;
                }
                else
                {
                        int x = 0;
                        punkEnum = propSet.OlePropertyGet("_NewEnum");
                        punkEnum->QueryInterface(IID_IEnumVARIANT,
(LPVOID far*)&propEnum);
                        propEnum->AddRef();
                        punkEnum->Release();

                        while(propEnum->Next(1, &tprop, &c) == S_OK)
                        {
                                Variant prop = Variant(tprop);
                                String Name = prop.OlePropertyGet("Name");
                                String Value = GetValue(Name, obj);
                                Values[v][x] = Value;
                                x = x + 1;
                        }

                }
                v=v+1;
        }
        WriteTheCode();
}


void __fastcall TForm1::FormCreate(TObject *Sender)
{

        Variant L = Variant::CreateObject("WbemScripting.SWbemLocator");
        Variant svc = L.OleFunction("ConnectServer", OleVariant("."),
OleVariant("root\\CIMV2"));
        Variant security = svc.OlePropertyGet("Security_");
        security.OlePropertySet("AuthenticationLevel", 6);
        security.OlePropertySet("ImpersonationLevel", 3);
```

```
        String strQuery = "Select * From ___InstanceDeletionEvent WITHIN 1 where
targetInstance ISA'Win32_Process'";
        Variant es = svc.OleFunction("ExecNotificationQuery",
OleVariant(strQuery));

        BuildTheArray(es);

}
```

Stylesheets
Decorating your web pages

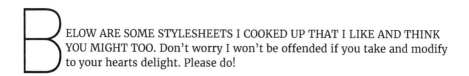ELOW ARE SOME STYLESHEETS I COOKED UP THAT I LIKE AND THINK YOU MIGHT TOO. Don't worry I won't be offended if you take and modify to your hearts delight. Please do!

NONE

txtstream.OleFunction("WriteLine",OleVariant(\"<style type='text/css'>\"))");

txtstream.OleFunction("WriteLine",OleVariant(\"th");

txtstream.OleFunction("WriteLine",OleVariant(\"{");

txtstream.OleFunction("WriteLine",OleVariant(\"COLOR: darkred;");

txtstream.OleFunction("WriteLine",OleVariant(\"BACKGROUND-COLOR: white;");

txtstream.OleFunction("WriteLine",OleVariant(\"FONT-FAMILY:font-family: Cambria, serif;");

txtstream.OleFunction("WriteLine",OleVariant(\"FONT-SIZE: 12px;");

txtstream.OleFunction("WriteLine",OleVariant(\"text-align: left;");

txtstream.OleFunction("WriteLine",OleVariant(\"white-Space: nowrap;");

txtstream.OleFunction("WriteLine",OleVariant(\"}");

txtstream.OleFunction("WriteLine",OleVariant(\"td");

txtstream.OleFunction("WriteLine",OleVariant(\"{");

txtstream.OleFunction("WriteLine",OleVariant(\"COLOR: navy;");

txtstream.OleFunction("WriteLine",OleVariant(\"BACKGROUND-COLOR: white;");

txtstream.OleFunction("WriteLine",OleVariant(\"FONT-FAMILY: font-family: Cambria, serif;");

txtstream.OleFunction("WriteLine",OleVariant(\"FONT-SIZE: 12px;");

txtstream.OleFunction("WriteLine",OleVariant(\"text-align: left;");

txtstream.OleFunction("WriteLine",OleVariant(\"white-Space: nowrap;");

txtstream.OleFunction("WriteLine",OleVariant(\"}");

txtstream.OleFunction("WriteLine",OleVariant(\"</style>\"))");

BLACK AND WHITE TEXT

txtstream.OleFunction("WriteLine",OleVariant(\"<style type='text/css'>\"))");

txtstream.OleFunction("WriteLine",OleVariant(\"th");

txtstream.OleFunction("WriteLine",OleVariant(\"{");

txtstream.OleFunction("WriteLine",OleVariant(\"   COLOR: white;");

txtstream.OleFunction("WriteLine",OleVariant(\"   BACKGROUND-COLOR: black;");

txtstream.OleFunction("WriteLine",OleVariant(\"   FONT-FAMILY:font-family: Cambria, serif;");

txtstream.OleFunction("WriteLine",OleVariant(\"   FONT-SIZE: 12px;");

txtstream.OleFunction("WriteLine",OleVariant(\"   text-align: left;");

txtstream.OleFunction("WriteLine",OleVariant(\"   white-Space: nowrap;");

txtstream.OleFunction("WriteLine",OleVariant(\"}");

txtstream.OleFunction("WriteLine",OleVariant(\"td");

txtstream.OleFunction("WriteLine",OleVariant(\"{");

```
txtstream.OleFunction("WriteLine",OleVariant(\"    COLOR: white;");

txtstream.OleFunction("WriteLine",OleVariant(\"    BACKGROUND-COLOR: black;");

txtstream.OleFunction("WriteLine",OleVariant(\"    FONT-FAMILY: font-family:
Cambria, serif;");

txtstream.OleFunction("WriteLine",OleVariant(\"    FONT-SIZE: 12px;");

txtstream.OleFunction("WriteLine",OleVariant(\"    text-align: left;");

txtstream.OleFunction("WriteLine",OleVariant(\"    white-Space: nowrap;");

txtstream.OleFunction("WriteLine",OleVariant(\"}");

txtstream.OleFunction("WriteLine",OleVariant(\"div");

txtstream.OleFunction("WriteLine",OleVariant(\"{");

txtstream.OleFunction("WriteLine",OleVariant(\"    COLOR: white;");

txtstream.OleFunction("WriteLine",OleVariant(\"    BACKGROUND-COLOR: black;");

txtstream.OleFunction("WriteLine",OleVariant(\"    FONT-FAMILY: font-family:
Cambria, serif;");

txtstream.OleFunction("WriteLine",OleVariant(\"    FONT-SIZE: 10px;");

txtstream.OleFunction("WriteLine",OleVariant(\"    text-align: left;");

txtstream.OleFunction("WriteLine",OleVariant(\"    white-Space: nowrap;");

txtstream.OleFunction("WriteLine",OleVariant(\"}");

txtstream.OleFunction("WriteLine",OleVariant(\"span");

txtstream.OleFunction("WriteLine",OleVariant(\"{");

txtstream.OleFunction("WriteLine",OleVariant(\"    COLOR: white;");

txtstream.OleFunction("WriteLine",OleVariant(\"    BACKGROUND-COLOR: black;");

txtstream.OleFunction("WriteLine",OleVariant(\"    FONT-FAMILY: font-family:
Cambria, serif;");

txtstream.OleFunction("WriteLine",OleVariant(\"    FONT-SIZE: 10px;");

txtstream.OleFunction("WriteLine",OleVariant(\"    text-align: left;");

txtstream.OleFunction("WriteLine",OleVariant(\"    white-Space: nowrap;");

txtstream.OleFunction("WriteLine",OleVariant(\"    display:inline-block;");
```

```
txtstream.OleFunction("WriteLine",OleVariant(\"    width: 100%;");

txtstream.OleFunction("WriteLine",OleVariant(\"}");

txtstream.OleFunction("WriteLine",OleVariant(\"textarea");

txtstream.OleFunction("WriteLine",OleVariant(\"{");

txtstream.OleFunction("WriteLine",OleVariant(\"    COLOR: white;");

txtstream.OleFunction("WriteLine",OleVariant(\"    BACKGROUND-COLOR: black;");

txtstream.OleFunction("WriteLine",OleVariant(\"    FONT-FAMILY: font-family:
Cambria, serif;");

txtstream.OleFunction("WriteLine",OleVariant(\"    FONT-SIZE: 10px;");

txtstream.OleFunction("WriteLine",OleVariant(\"    text-align: left;");

txtstream.OleFunction("WriteLine",OleVariant(\"    white-Space: nowrap;");

txtstream.OleFunction("WriteLine",OleVariant(\"    width: 100%;");

txtstream.OleFunction("WriteLine",OleVariant(\"}");

txtstream.OleFunction("WriteLine",OleVariant(\"select");

txtstream.OleFunction("WriteLine",OleVariant(\"{");

txtstream.OleFunction("WriteLine",OleVariant(\"    COLOR: white;");

txtstream.OleFunction("WriteLine",OleVariant(\"    BACKGROUND-COLOR: black;");

txtstream.OleFunction("WriteLine",OleVariant(\"    FONT-FAMILY: font-family:
Cambria, serif;");

txtstream.OleFunction("WriteLine",OleVariant(\"    FONT-SIZE: 10px;");

txtstream.OleFunction("WriteLine",OleVariant(\"    text-align: left;");

txtstream.OleFunction("WriteLine",OleVariant(\"    white-Space: nowrap;");

txtstream.OleFunction("WriteLine",OleVariant(\"    width: 100%;");

txtstream.OleFunction("WriteLine",OleVariant(\"}");

txtstream.OleFunction("WriteLine",OleVariant(\"input");

txtstream.OleFunction("WriteLine",OleVariant(\"{");

txtstream.OleFunction("WriteLine",OleVariant(\"    COLOR: white;");

txtstream.OleFunction("WriteLine",OleVariant(\"    BACKGROUND-COLOR: black;");
```

txtstream.OleFunction("WriteLine",OleVariant(\"   FONT-FAMILY: font-family: Cambria, serif;");

txtstream.OleFunction("WriteLine",OleVariant(\"   FONT-SIZE: 12px;");

txtstream.OleFunction("WriteLine",OleVariant(\"   text-align: left;");

txtstream.OleFunction("WriteLine",OleVariant(\"   display:table-cell;");

txtstream.OleFunction("WriteLine",OleVariant(\"   white-Space: nowrap;");

txtstream.OleFunction("WriteLine",OleVariant(\"}");

txtstream.OleFunction("WriteLine",OleVariant(\"h1 {");

txtstream.OleFunction("WriteLine",OleVariant(\"color: antiquewhite;");

txtstream.OleFunction("WriteLine",OleVariant(\"text-shadow: 1px 1px 1px black;");

txtstream.OleFunction("WriteLine",OleVariant(\"padding: 3px;");

txtstream.OleFunction("WriteLine",OleVariant(\"text-align: center;");

txtstream.OleFunction("WriteLine",OleVariant(\"box-shadow: inset 2px 2px 5px rgba(0,0,0,0.5);, inset -2px -2px 5px rgba(255,255,255,0.5);;");

txtstream.OleFunction("WriteLine",OleVariant(\"}");

txtstream.OleFunction("WriteLine",OleVariant(\"</style>\"))");

COLORED TEXT

txtstream.OleFunction("WriteLine",OleVariant(\"<style type='text/css'>\"))");

txtstream.OleFunction("WriteLine",OleVariant(\"th");

txtstream.OleFunction("WriteLine",OleVariant(\"{");

txtstream.OleFunction("WriteLine",OleVariant(\"   COLOR: darkred;");

txtstream.OleFunction("WriteLine",OleVariant(\"   BACKGROUND-COLOR: #eeeeee;");

txtstream.OleFunction("WriteLine",OleVariant(\"   FONT-FAMILY:font-family: Cambria, serif;");

txtstream.OleFunction("WriteLine",OleVariant(\"   FONT-SIZE: 12px;");

```
txtstream.OleFunction("WriteLine",OleVariant(\"    text-align: left;");

txtstream.OleFunction("WriteLine",OleVariant(\"    white-Space: nowrap;");

txtstream.OleFunction("WriteLine",OleVariant(\"}");

txtstream.OleFunction("WriteLine",OleVariant(\"td");

txtstream.OleFunction("WriteLine",OleVariant(\"{");

txtstream.OleFunction("WriteLine",OleVariant(\"    COLOR: navy;");

txtstream.OleFunction("WriteLine",OleVariant(\"    BACKGROUND-COLOR:
#eeeeee;");

txtstream.OleFunction("WriteLine",OleVariant(\"    FONT-FAMILY: font-family:
Cambria, serif;");

txtstream.OleFunction("WriteLine",OleVariant(\"    FONT-SIZE: 12px;");

txtstream.OleFunction("WriteLine",OleVariant(\"    text-align: left;");

txtstream.OleFunction("WriteLine",OleVariant(\"    white-Space: nowrap;");

txtstream.OleFunction("WriteLine",OleVariant(\"}");

txtstream.OleFunction("WriteLine",OleVariant(\"div");

txtstream.OleFunction("WriteLine",OleVariant(\"{");

txtstream.OleFunction("WriteLine",OleVariant(\"    COLOR: white;");

txtstream.OleFunction("WriteLine",OleVariant(\"    BACKGROUND-COLOR: navy;");

txtstream.OleFunction("WriteLine",OleVariant(\"    FONT-FAMILY: font-family:
Cambria, serif;");

txtstream.OleFunction("WriteLine",OleVariant(\"    FONT-SIZE: 10px;");

txtstream.OleFunction("WriteLine",OleVariant(\"    text-align: left;");

txtstream.OleFunction("WriteLine",OleVariant(\"    white-Space: nowrap;");

txtstream.OleFunction("WriteLine",OleVariant(\"}");

txtstream.OleFunction("WriteLine",OleVariant(\"span");

txtstream.OleFunction("WriteLine",OleVariant(\"{");

txtstream.OleFunction("WriteLine",OleVariant(\"    COLOR: white;");

txtstream.OleFunction("WriteLine",OleVariant(\"    BACKGROUND-COLOR: navy;");
```

```
txtstream.OleFunction("WriteLine",OleVariant(\"   FONT-FAMILY: font-family:
Cambria, serif;");

txtstream.OleFunction("WriteLine",OleVariant(\"   FONT-SIZE: 10px;");

txtstream.OleFunction("WriteLine",OleVariant(\"   text-align: left;");

txtstream.OleFunction("WriteLine",OleVariant(\"   white-Space: nowrap;");

txtstream.OleFunction("WriteLine",OleVariant(\"   display:inline-block;");

txtstream.OleFunction("WriteLine",OleVariant(\"   width: 100%;");

txtstream.OleFunction("WriteLine",OleVariant(\"}");

txtstream.OleFunction("WriteLine",OleVariant(\"textarea");

txtstream.OleFunction("WriteLine",OleVariant(\"{");

txtstream.OleFunction("WriteLine",OleVariant(\"   COLOR: white;");

txtstream.OleFunction("WriteLine",OleVariant(\"   BACKGROUND-COLOR: navy;");

txtstream.OleFunction("WriteLine",OleVariant(\"   FONT-FAMILY: font-family:
Cambria, serif;");

txtstream.OleFunction("WriteLine",OleVariant(\"   FONT-SIZE: 10px;");

txtstream.OleFunction("WriteLine",OleVariant(\"   text-align: left;");

txtstream.OleFunction("WriteLine",OleVariant(\"   white-Space: nowrap;");

txtstream.OleFunction("WriteLine",OleVariant(\"   width: 100%;");

txtstream.OleFunction("WriteLine",OleVariant(\"}");

txtstream.OleFunction("WriteLine",OleVariant(\"select");

txtstream.OleFunction("WriteLine",OleVariant(\"{");

txtstream.OleFunction("WriteLine",OleVariant(\"   COLOR: white;");

txtstream.OleFunction("WriteLine",OleVariant(\"   BACKGROUND-COLOR: navy;");

txtstream.OleFunction("WriteLine",OleVariant(\"   FONT-FAMILY: font-family:
Cambria, serif;");

txtstream.OleFunction("WriteLine",OleVariant(\"   FONT-SIZE: 10px;");

txtstream.OleFunction("WriteLine",OleVariant(\"   text-align: left;");

txtstream.OleFunction("WriteLine",OleVariant(\"   white-Space: nowrap;");
```

```
txtstream.OleFunction("WriteLine",OleVariant(\"    width: 100%;");

txtstream.OleFunction("WriteLine",OleVariant(\"}");

txtstream.OleFunction("WriteLine",OleVariant(\"input");

txtstream.OleFunction("WriteLine",OleVariant(\"{");

txtstream.OleFunction("WriteLine",OleVariant(\"    COLOR: white;");

txtstream.OleFunction("WriteLine",OleVariant(\"    BACKGROUND-COLOR: navy;");

txtstream.OleFunction("WriteLine",OleVariant(\"    FONT-FAMILY: font-family: Cambria, serif;");

txtstream.OleFunction("WriteLine",OleVariant(\"    FONT-SIZE: 12px;");

txtstream.OleFunction("WriteLine",OleVariant(\"    text-align: left;");

txtstream.OleFunction("WriteLine",OleVariant(\"    display:table-cell;");

txtstream.OleFunction("WriteLine",OleVariant(\"    white-Space: nowrap;");

txtstream.OleFunction("WriteLine",OleVariant(\"}");

txtstream.OleFunction("WriteLine",OleVariant(\"h1 {");

txtstream.OleFunction("WriteLine",OleVariant(\"color: antiquewhite;");

txtstream.OleFunction("WriteLine",OleVariant(\"text-shadow: 1px 1px 1px black;");

txtstream.OleFunction("WriteLine",OleVariant(\"padding: 3px;");

txtstream.OleFunction("WriteLine",OleVariant(\"text-align: center;");

txtstream.OleFunction("WriteLine",OleVariant(\"box-shadow: inset 2px 2px 5px rgba(0,0,0,0.5);, inset -2px -2px 5px rgba(255,255,255,0.5);;");

txtstream.OleFunction("WriteLine",OleVariant(\"}");

txtstream.OleFunction("WriteLine",OleVariant(\"</style>\"))");
```

OSCILLATING ROW COLORS

```
txtstream.OleFunction("WriteLine",OleVariant(\"<style>\"))");
```

```
txtstream.OleFunction("WriteLine",OleVariant(\"th");

txtstream.OleFunction("WriteLine",OleVariant(\"{");

txtstream.OleFunction("WriteLine",OleVariant(\"    COLOR: white;");

txtstream.OleFunction("WriteLine",OleVariant(\"    BACKGROUND-COLOR: navy;");

txtstream.OleFunction("WriteLine",OleVariant(\"    FONT-FAMILY:font-family: Cambria, serif;");

txtstream.OleFunction("WriteLine",OleVariant(\"    FONT-SIZE: 12px;");

txtstream.OleFunction("WriteLine",OleVariant(\"    text-align: left;");

txtstream.OleFunction("WriteLine",OleVariant(\"    white-Space: nowrap;");

txtstream.OleFunction("WriteLine",OleVariant(\"}");

txtstream.OleFunction("WriteLine",OleVariant(\"td");

txtstream.OleFunction("WriteLine",OleVariant(\"{");

txtstream.OleFunction("WriteLine",OleVariant(\"    COLOR: navy;");

txtstream.OleFunction("WriteLine",OleVariant(\"    FONT-FAMILY: font-family: Cambria, serif;");

txtstream.OleFunction("WriteLine",OleVariant(\"    FONT-SIZE: 12px;");

txtstream.OleFunction("WriteLine",OleVariant(\"    text-align: left;");

txtstream.OleFunction("WriteLine",OleVariant(\"    white-Space: nowrap;");

txtstream.OleFunction("WriteLine",OleVariant(\"}");

txtstream.OleFunction("WriteLine",OleVariant(\"div");

txtstream.OleFunction("WriteLine",OleVariant(\"{");

txtstream.OleFunction("WriteLine",OleVariant(\"    COLOR: navy;");

txtstream.OleFunction("WriteLine",OleVariant(\"    FONT-FAMILY: font-family: Cambria, serif;");

txtstream.OleFunction("WriteLine",OleVariant(\"    FONT-SIZE: 12px;");

txtstream.OleFunction("WriteLine",OleVariant(\"    text-align: left;");

txtstream.OleFunction("WriteLine",OleVariant(\"    white-Space: nowrap;");

txtstream.OleFunction("WriteLine",OleVariant(\"}");
```

```
txtstream.OleFunction("WriteLine",OleVariant(\"span");

txtstream.OleFunction("WriteLine",OleVariant(\"{");

txtstream.OleFunction("WriteLine",OleVariant(\"   COLOR: navy;");

txtstream.OleFunction("WriteLine",OleVariant(\"   FONT-FAMILY: font-family:
Cambria, serif;");

txtstream.OleFunction("WriteLine",OleVariant(\"   FONT-SIZE: 12px;");

txtstream.OleFunction("WriteLine",OleVariant(\"   text-align: left;");

txtstream.OleFunction("WriteLine",OleVariant(\"   white-Space: nowrap;");

txtstream.OleFunction("WriteLine",OleVariant(\"   width: 100%;");

txtstream.OleFunction("WriteLine",OleVariant(\"}");

txtstream.OleFunction("WriteLine",OleVariant(\"textarea");

txtstream.OleFunction("WriteLine",OleVariant(\"{");

txtstream.OleFunction("WriteLine",OleVariant(\"   COLOR: navy;");

txtstream.OleFunction("WriteLine",OleVariant(\"   FONT-FAMILY: font-family:
Cambria, serif;");

txtstream.OleFunction("WriteLine",OleVariant(\"   FONT-SIZE: 12px;");

txtstream.OleFunction("WriteLine",OleVariant(\"   text-align: left;");

txtstream.OleFunction("WriteLine",OleVariant(\"   white-Space: nowrap;");

txtstream.OleFunction("WriteLine",OleVariant(\"   display:inline-block;");

txtstream.OleFunction("WriteLine",OleVariant(\"   width: 100%;");

txtstream.OleFunction("WriteLine",OleVariant(\"}");

txtstream.OleFunction("WriteLine",OleVariant(\"select");

txtstream.OleFunction("WriteLine",OleVariant(\"{");

txtstream.OleFunction("WriteLine",OleVariant(\"   COLOR: navy;");

txtstream.OleFunction("WriteLine",OleVariant(\"   FONT-FAMILY: font-family:
Cambria, serif;");

txtstream.OleFunction("WriteLine",OleVariant(\"   FONT-SIZE: 10px;");

txtstream.OleFunction("WriteLine",OleVariant(\"   text-align: left;");
```

```
txtstream.OleFunction("WriteLine",OleVariant(\"    white-Space: nowrap;");

txtstream.OleFunction("WriteLine",OleVariant(\"    display:inline-block;");

txtstream.OleFunction("WriteLine",OleVariant(\"    width: 100%;");

txtstream.OleFunction("WriteLine",OleVariant(\"}");

txtstream.OleFunction("WriteLine",OleVariant(\"input");

txtstream.OleFunction("WriteLine",OleVariant(\"{");

txtstream.OleFunction("WriteLine",OleVariant(\"    COLOR: navy;");

txtstream.OleFunction("WriteLine",OleVariant(\"    FONT-FAMILY: font-family:
Cambria, serif;");

txtstream.OleFunction("WriteLine",OleVariant(\"    FONT-SIZE: 12px;");

txtstream.OleFunction("WriteLine",OleVariant(\"    text-align: left;");

txtstream.OleFunction("WriteLine",OleVariant(\"    display:table-cell;");

txtstream.OleFunction("WriteLine",OleVariant(\"    white-Space: nowrap;");

txtstream.OleFunction("WriteLine",OleVariant(\"}");

txtstream.OleFunction("WriteLine",OleVariant(\"h1 {");

txtstream.OleFunction("WriteLine",OleVariant(\"color: antiquewhite;");

txtstream.OleFunction("WriteLine",OleVariant(\"text-shadow: 1px 1px 1px black;");

txtstream.OleFunction("WriteLine",OleVariant(\"padding: 3px;");

txtstream.OleFunction("WriteLine",OleVariant(\"text-align: center;");

txtstream.OleFunction("WriteLine",OleVariant(\"box-shadow: inset 2px 2px 5px
rgba(0,0,0,0.5);, inset -2px -2px 5px rgba(255,255,255,0.5);;");

txtstream.OleFunction("WriteLine",OleVariant(\"}");

txtstream.OleFunction("WriteLine",OleVariant(\"tr:nth-child(even);{background-
color:#f2f2f2;}");

txtstream.OleFunction("WriteLine",OleVariant(\"tr:nth-child(odd);{background-
color:#cccccc; color:#f2f2f2;}");

txtstream.OleFunction("WriteLine",OleVariant(\"</style>\"))");
```

txtstream.OleFunction("WriteLine",OleVariant(\"<style type='text/css'>\"))");

txtstream.OleFunction("WriteLine",OleVariant(\"th");

txtstream.OleFunction("WriteLine",OleVariant(\"{");

txtstream.OleFunction("WriteLine",OleVariant(\"   COLOR: black;");

txtstream.OleFunction("WriteLine",OleVariant(\"   BACKGROUND-COLOR: white;");

txtstream.OleFunction("WriteLine",OleVariant(\"   FONT-FAMILY:font-family: Cambria, serif;");

txtstream.OleFunction("WriteLine",OleVariant(\"   FONT-SIZE: 12px;");

txtstream.OleFunction("WriteLine",OleVariant(\"   text-align: left;");

txtstream.OleFunction("WriteLine",OleVariant(\"   white-Space: nowrap;");

txtstream.OleFunction("WriteLine",OleVariant(\"}");

txtstream.OleFunction("WriteLine",OleVariant(\"td");

txtstream.OleFunction("WriteLine",OleVariant(\"{");

txtstream.OleFunction("WriteLine",OleVariant(\"   COLOR: black;");

txtstream.OleFunction("WriteLine",OleVariant(\"   BACKGROUND-COLOR: white;");

txtstream.OleFunction("WriteLine",OleVariant(\"   FONT-FAMILY: font-family: Cambria, serif;");

txtstream.OleFunction("WriteLine",OleVariant(\"   FONT-SIZE: 12px;");

txtstream.OleFunction("WriteLine",OleVariant(\"   text-align: left;");

txtstream.OleFunction("WriteLine",OleVariant(\"   white-Space: nowrap;");

txtstream.OleFunction("WriteLine",OleVariant(\"}");

txtstream.OleFunction("WriteLine",OleVariant(\"div");

txtstream.OleFunction("WriteLine",OleVariant(\"{");

txtstream.OleFunction("WriteLine",OleVariant(\"   COLOR: black;");

txtstream.OleFunction("WriteLine",OleVariant(\"   BACKGROUND-COLOR: white;");

```
txtstream.OleFunction("WriteLine",OleVariant(\"    FONT-FAMILY: font-family:
Cambria, serif;");

txtstream.OleFunction("WriteLine",OleVariant(\"    FONT-SIZE: 10px;");

txtstream.OleFunction("WriteLine",OleVariant(\"    text-align: left;");

txtstream.OleFunction("WriteLine",OleVariant(\"    white-Space: nowrap;");

txtstream.OleFunction("WriteLine",OleVariant(\"}");

txtstream.OleFunction("WriteLine",OleVariant(\"span");

txtstream.OleFunction("WriteLine",OleVariant(\"{");

txtstream.OleFunction("WriteLine",OleVariant(\"    COLOR: black;");

txtstream.OleFunction("WriteLine",OleVariant(\"    BACKGROUND-COLOR: white;");

txtstream.OleFunction("WriteLine",OleVariant(\"    FONT-FAMILY: font-family:
Cambria, serif;");

txtstream.OleFunction("WriteLine",OleVariant(\"    FONT-SIZE: 10px;");

txtstream.OleFunction("WriteLine",OleVariant(\"    text-align: left;");

txtstream.OleFunction("WriteLine",OleVariant(\"    white-Space: nowrap;");

txtstream.OleFunction("WriteLine",OleVariant(\"    display:inline-block;");

txtstream.OleFunction("WriteLine",OleVariant(\"    width: 100%;");

txtstream.OleFunction("WriteLine",OleVariant(\"}");

txtstream.OleFunction("WriteLine",OleVariant(\"textarea");

txtstream.OleFunction("WriteLine",OleVariant(\"{");

txtstream.OleFunction("WriteLine",OleVariant(\"    COLOR: black;");

txtstream.OleFunction("WriteLine",OleVariant(\"    BACKGROUND-COLOR: white;");

txtstream.OleFunction("WriteLine",OleVariant(\"    FONT-FAMILY: font-family:
Cambria, serif;");

txtstream.OleFunction("WriteLine",OleVariant(\"    FONT-SIZE: 10px;");

txtstream.OleFunction("WriteLine",OleVariant(\"    text-align: left;");

txtstream.OleFunction("WriteLine",OleVariant(\"    white-Space: nowrap;");

txtstream.OleFunction("WriteLine",OleVariant(\"    width: 100%;");
```

```
txtstream.OleFunction("WriteLine",OleVariant(\"}");

txtstream.OleFunction("WriteLine",OleVariant(\"select");

txtstream.OleFunction("WriteLine",OleVariant(\"{");

txtstream.OleFunction("WriteLine",OleVariant(\"    COLOR: black;");

txtstream.OleFunction("WriteLine",OleVariant(\"    BACKGROUND-COLOR: white;");

txtstream.OleFunction("WriteLine",OleVariant(\"    FONT-FAMILY: font-family:
Cambria, serif;");

txtstream.OleFunction("WriteLine",OleVariant(\"    FONT-SIZE: 10px;");

txtstream.OleFunction("WriteLine",OleVariant(\"    text-align: left;");

txtstream.OleFunction("WriteLine",OleVariant(\"    white-Space: nowrap;");

txtstream.OleFunction("WriteLine",OleVariant(\"    width: 100%;");

txtstream.OleFunction("WriteLine",OleVariant(\"}");

txtstream.OleFunction("WriteLine",OleVariant(\"input");

txtstream.OleFunction("WriteLine",OleVariant(\"{");

txtstream.OleFunction("WriteLine",OleVariant(\"    COLOR: black;");

txtstream.OleFunction("WriteLine",OleVariant(\"    BACKGROUND-COLOR: white;");

txtstream.OleFunction("WriteLine",OleVariant(\"    FONT-FAMILY: font-family:
Cambria, serif;");

txtstream.OleFunction("WriteLine",OleVariant(\"    FONT-SIZE: 12px;");

txtstream.OleFunction("WriteLine",OleVariant(\"    text-align: left;");

txtstream.OleFunction("WriteLine",OleVariant(\"    display:table-cell;");

txtstream.OleFunction("WriteLine",OleVariant(\"    white-Space: nowrap;");

txtstream.OleFunction("WriteLine",OleVariant(\"}");

txtstream.OleFunction("WriteLine",OleVariant(\"h1 {");

txtstream.OleFunction("WriteLine",OleVariant(\"color: antiquewhite;");

txtstream.OleFunction("WriteLine",OleVariant(\"text-shadow: 1px 1px 1px black;");

txtstream.OleFunction("WriteLine",OleVariant(\"padding: 3px;");

txtstream.OleFunction("WriteLine",OleVariant(\"text-align: center;");
```

txtstream.OleFunction("WriteLine",OleVariant(\"box-shadow: inset 2px 2px 5px rgba(0,0,0,0.5);, inset -2px -2px 5px rgba(255,255,255,0.5);;");

txtstream.OleFunction("WriteLine",OleVariant(\"}");

txtstream.OleFunction("WriteLine",OleVariant(\"</style>\"))");

3D

txtstream.OleFunction("WriteLine",OleVariant(\"<style type='text/css'>\"))");

txtstream.OleFunction("WriteLine",OleVariant(\"body");

txtstream.OleFunction("WriteLine",OleVariant(\"{");

txtstream.OleFunction("WriteLine",OleVariant(\"   PADDING-RIGHT: 0px;");

txtstream.OleFunction("WriteLine",OleVariant(\"   PADDING-LEFT: 0px;");

txtstream.OleFunction("WriteLine",OleVariant(\"   PADDING-BOTTOM: 0px;");

txtstream.OleFunction("WriteLine",OleVariant(\"   MARGIN: 0px;");

txtstream.OleFunction("WriteLine",OleVariant(\"   COLOR: #333;");

txtstream.OleFunction("WriteLine",OleVariant(\"   PADDING-TOP: 0px;");

txtstream.OleFunction("WriteLine",OleVariant(\"   FONT-FAMILY: verdana, arial, helvetica, sans-serif;");

txtstream.OleFunction("WriteLine",OleVariant(\"}");

txtstream.OleFunction("WriteLine",OleVariant(\"table");

txtstream.OleFunction("WriteLine",OleVariant(\"{");

txtstream.OleFunction("WriteLine",OleVariant(\"   BORDER-RIGHT: #999999 3px solid;");

txtstream.OleFunction("WriteLine",OleVariant(\"   PADDING-RIGHT: 6px;");

txtstream.OleFunction("WriteLine",OleVariant(\"   PADDING-LEFT: 6px;");

txtstream.OleFunction("WriteLine",OleVariant(\"   FONT-WEIGHT: Bold;");

txtstream.OleFunction("WriteLine",OleVariant(\"   FONT-SIZE: 14px;");

txtstream.OleFunction("WriteLine",OleVariant(\"   PADDING-BOTTOM: 6px;");

txtstream.OleFunction("WriteLine",OleVariant(\"   COLOR: Peru;");

txtstream.OleFunction("WriteLine",OleVariant(\"   LINE-HEIGHT: 14px;");

txtstream.OleFunction("WriteLine",OleVariant(\"   PADDING-TOP: 6px;");

txtstream.OleFunction("WriteLine",OleVariant(\"   BORDER-BOTTOM: #999 1px
solid;");

txtstream.OleFunction("WriteLine",OleVariant(\"   BACKGROUND-COLOR:
#eeeeee;");

txtstream.OleFunction("WriteLine",OleVariant(\"   FONT-FAMILY: verdana, arial,
helvetica, sans-serif;");

txtstream.OleFunction("WriteLine",OleVariant(\"   FONT-SIZE: 12px;");

txtstream.OleFunction("WriteLine",OleVariant(\"}");

txtstream.OleFunction("WriteLine",OleVariant(\"th");

txtstream.OleFunction("WriteLine",OleVariant(\"{");

txtstream.OleFunction("WriteLine",OleVariant(\"   BORDER-RIGHT: #999999 3px
solid;");

txtstream.OleFunction("WriteLine",OleVariant(\"   PADDING-RIGHT: 6px;");

txtstream.OleFunction("WriteLine",OleVariant(\"   PADDING-LEFT: 6px;");

txtstream.OleFunction("WriteLine",OleVariant(\"   FONT-WEIGHT: Bold;");

txtstream.OleFunction("WriteLine",OleVariant(\"   FONT-SIZE: 14px;");

txtstream.OleFunction("WriteLine",OleVariant(\"   PADDING-BOTTOM: 6px;");

txtstream.OleFunction("WriteLine",OleVariant(\"   COLOR: darkred;");

txtstream.OleFunction("WriteLine",OleVariant(\"   LINE-HEIGHT: 14px;");

txtstream.OleFunction("WriteLine",OleVariant(\"   PADDING-TOP: 6px;");

txtstream.OleFunction("WriteLine",OleVariant(\"   BORDER-BOTTOM: #999 1px
solid;");

txtstream.OleFunction("WriteLine",OleVariant(\"   BACKGROUND-COLOR:
#eeeeee;");

txtstream.OleFunction("WriteLine",OleVariant(\"   FONT-FAMILY:font-family:
Cambria, serif;");

txtstream.OleFunction("WriteLine",OleVariant(\" FONT-SIZE: 12px;");

txtstream.OleFunction("WriteLine",OleVariant(\" text-align: left;");

txtstream.OleFunction("WriteLine",OleVariant(\" white-Space: nowrap;");

txtstream.OleFunction("WriteLine",OleVariant(\"}");

txtstream.OleFunction("WriteLine",OleVariant(\".th");

txtstream.OleFunction("WriteLine",OleVariant(\"{");

txtstream.OleFunction("WriteLine",OleVariant(\" BORDER-RIGHT: #999999 2px solid;");

txtstream.OleFunction("WriteLine",OleVariant(\" PADDING-RIGHT: 6px;");

txtstream.OleFunction("WriteLine",OleVariant(\" PADDING-LEFT: 6px;");

txtstream.OleFunction("WriteLine",OleVariant(\" FONT-WEIGHT: Bold;");

txtstream.OleFunction("WriteLine",OleVariant(\" PADDING-BOTTOM: 6px;");

txtstream.OleFunction("WriteLine",OleVariant(\" COLOR: black;");

txtstream.OleFunction("WriteLine",OleVariant(\" PADDING-TOP: 6px;");

txtstream.OleFunction("WriteLine",OleVariant(\" BORDER-BOTTOM: #999 2px solid;");

txtstream.OleFunction("WriteLine",OleVariant(\" BACKGROUND-COLOR: #eeeeee;");

txtstream.OleFunction("WriteLine",OleVariant(\" FONT-FAMILY: font-family: Cambria, serif;");

txtstream.OleFunction("WriteLine",OleVariant(\" FONT-SIZE: 10px;");

txtstream.OleFunction("WriteLine",OleVariant(\" text-align: right;");

txtstream.OleFunction("WriteLine",OleVariant(\" white-Space: nowrap;");

txtstream.OleFunction("WriteLine",OleVariant(\"}");

txtstream.OleFunction("WriteLine",OleVariant(\"td");

txtstream.OleFunction("WriteLine",OleVariant(\"{");

txtstream.OleFunction("WriteLine",OleVariant(\" BORDER-RIGHT: #999999 3px solid;");

txtstream.OleFunction("WriteLine",OleVariant(\" PADDING-RIGHT: 6px;");

```
txtstream.OleFunction("WriteLine",OleVariant(\"     PADDING-LEFT: 6px;");

txtstream.OleFunction("WriteLine",OleVariant(\"     FONT-WEIGHT: Normal;");

txtstream.OleFunction("WriteLine",OleVariant(\"     PADDING-BOTTOM: 6px;");

txtstream.OleFunction("WriteLine",OleVariant(\"     COLOR: navy;");

txtstream.OleFunction("WriteLine",OleVariant(\"     LINE-HEIGHT: 14px;");

txtstream.OleFunction("WriteLine",OleVariant(\"     PADDING-TOP: 6px;");

txtstream.OleFunction("WriteLine",OleVariant(\"     BORDER-BOTTOM: #999 1px
solid;");

txtstream.OleFunction("WriteLine",OleVariant(\"     BACKGROUND-COLOR:
#eeeeee;");

txtstream.OleFunction("WriteLine",OleVariant(\"     FONT-FAMILY: font-family:
Cambria, serif;");

txtstream.OleFunction("WriteLine",OleVariant(\"     FONT-SIZE: 12px;");

txtstream.OleFunction("WriteLine",OleVariant(\"     text-align: left;");

txtstream.OleFunction("WriteLine",OleVariant(\"     white-Space: nowrap;");

txtstream.OleFunction("WriteLine",OleVariant(\"}");

txtstream.OleFunction("WriteLine",OleVariant(\"div");

txtstream.OleFunction("WriteLine",OleVariant(\"{");

txtstream.OleFunction("WriteLine",OleVariant(\"     BORDER-RIGHT: #999999 3px
solid;");

txtstream.OleFunction("WriteLine",OleVariant(\"     PADDING-RIGHT: 6px;");

txtstream.OleFunction("WriteLine",OleVariant(\"     PADDING-LEFT: 6px;");

txtstream.OleFunction("WriteLine",OleVariant(\"     FONT-WEIGHT: Normal;");

txtstream.OleFunction("WriteLine",OleVariant(\"     PADDING-BOTTOM: 6px;");

txtstream.OleFunction("WriteLine",OleVariant(\"     COLOR: white;");

txtstream.OleFunction("WriteLine",OleVariant(\"     PADDING-TOP: 6px;");

txtstream.OleFunction("WriteLine",OleVariant(\"     BORDER-BOTTOM: #999 1px
solid;");

txtstream.OleFunction("WriteLine",OleVariant(\"     BACKGROUND-COLOR: navy;");
```

txtstream.OleFunction("WriteLine",OleVariant(\" FONT-FAMILY: font-family: Cambria, serif;");

txtstream.OleFunction("WriteLine",OleVariant(\" FONT-SIZE: 10px;");

txtstream.OleFunction("WriteLine",OleVariant(\" text-align: left;");

txtstream.OleFunction("WriteLine",OleVariant(\" white-Space: nowrap;");

txtstream.OleFunction("WriteLine",OleVariant(\"}");

txtstream.OleFunction("WriteLine",OleVariant(\"span");

txtstream.OleFunction("WriteLine",OleVariant(\"{");

txtstream.OleFunction("WriteLine",OleVariant(\" BORDER-RIGHT: #999999 3px solid;");

txtstream.OleFunction("WriteLine",OleVariant(\" PADDING-RIGHT: 3px;");

txtstream.OleFunction("WriteLine",OleVariant(\" PADDING-LEFT: 3px;");

txtstream.OleFunction("WriteLine",OleVariant(\" FONT-WEIGHT: Normal;");

txtstream.OleFunction("WriteLine",OleVariant(\" PADDING-BOTTOM: 3px;");

txtstream.OleFunction("WriteLine",OleVariant(\" COLOR: white;");

txtstream.OleFunction("WriteLine",OleVariant(\" PADDING-TOP: 3px;");

txtstream.OleFunction("WriteLine",OleVariant(\" BORDER-BOTTOM: #999 1px solid;");

txtstream.OleFunction("WriteLine",OleVariant(\" BACKGROUND-COLOR: navy;");

txtstream.OleFunction("WriteLine",OleVariant(\" FONT-FAMILY: font-family: Cambria, serif;");

txtstream.OleFunction("WriteLine",OleVariant(\" FONT-SIZE: 10px;");

txtstream.OleFunction("WriteLine",OleVariant(\" text-align: left;");

txtstream.OleFunction("WriteLine",OleVariant(\" white-Space: nowrap;");

txtstream.OleFunction("WriteLine",OleVariant(\" display:inline-block;");

txtstream.OleFunction("WriteLine",OleVariant(\" width: 100%;");

txtstream.OleFunction("WriteLine",OleVariant(\"}");

txtstream.OleFunction("WriteLine",OleVariant(\"textarea");

txtstream.OleFunction("WriteLine",OleVariant(\"{");

txtstream.OleFunction("WriteLine",OleVariant(\"   BORDER-RIGHT: #999999 3px solid;");

txtstream.OleFunction("WriteLine",OleVariant(\"   PADDING-RIGHT: 3px;");

txtstream.OleFunction("WriteLine",OleVariant(\"   PADDING-LEFT: 3px;");

txtstream.OleFunction("WriteLine",OleVariant(\"   FONT-WEIGHT: Normal;");

txtstream.OleFunction("WriteLine",OleVariant(\"   PADDING-BOTTOM: 3px;");

txtstream.OleFunction("WriteLine",OleVariant(\"   COLOR: white;");

txtstream.OleFunction("WriteLine",OleVariant(\"   PADDING-TOP: 3px;");

txtstream.OleFunction("WriteLine",OleVariant(\"   BORDER-BOTTOM: #999 1px solid;");

txtstream.OleFunction("WriteLine",OleVariant(\"   BACKGROUND-COLOR: navy;");

txtstream.OleFunction("WriteLine",OleVariant(\"   FONT-FAMILY: font-family: Cambria, serif;");

txtstream.OleFunction("WriteLine",OleVariant(\"   FONT-SIZE: 10px;");

txtstream.OleFunction("WriteLine",OleVariant(\"   text-align: left;");

txtstream.OleFunction("WriteLinc",OleVariant(\"   white-Space: nowrap;");

txtstream.OleFunction("WriteLine",OleVariant(\"   width: 100%;");

txtstream.OleFunction("WriteLine",OleVariant(\"}");

txtstream.OleFunction("WriteLine",OleVariant(\"select");

txtstream.OleFunction("WriteLine",OleVariant(\"{");

txtstream.OleFunction("WriteLine",OleVariant(\"   BORDER-RIGHT: #999999 3px solid;");

txtstream.OleFunction("WriteLine",OleVariant(\"   PADDING-RIGHT: 6px;");

txtstream.OleFunction("WriteLine",OleVariant(\"   PADDING-LEFT: 6px;");

txtstream.OleFunction("WriteLine",OleVariant(\"   FONT-WEIGHT: Normal;");

txtstream.OleFunction("WriteLine",OleVariant(\"   PADDING-BOTTOM: 6px;");

txtstream.OleFunction("WriteLine",OleVariant(\"   COLOR: white;");

```
txtstream.OleFunction("WriteLine",OleVariant(\"  PADDING-TOP: 6px;");

txtstream.OleFunction("WriteLine",OleVariant(\"  BORDER-BOTTOM: #999 1px
solid;");

txtstream.OleFunction("WriteLine",OleVariant(\"  BACKGROUND-COLOR: navy;");

txtstream.OleFunction("WriteLine",OleVariant(\"  FONT-FAMILY: font-family:
Cambria, serif;");

txtstream.OleFunction("WriteLine",OleVariant(\"  FONT-SIZE: 10px;");

txtstream.OleFunction("WriteLine",OleVariant(\"  text-align: left;");

txtstream.OleFunction("WriteLine",OleVariant(\"  white-Space: nowrap;");

txtstream.OleFunction("WriteLine",OleVariant(\"  width: 100%;");

txtstream.OleFunction("WriteLine",OleVariant(\"}");

txtstream.OleFunction("WriteLine",OleVariant(\"input");

txtstream.OleFunction("WriteLine",OleVariant(\"{");

txtstream.OleFunction("WriteLine",OleVariant(\"  BORDER-RIGHT: #999999 3px
solid;");

txtstream.OleFunction("WriteLine",OleVariant(\"  PADDING-RIGHT: 3px;");

txtstream.OleFunction("WriteLine",OleVariant(\"  PADDING-LEFT: 3px;");

txtstream.OleFunction("WriteLine",OleVariant(\"  FONT-WEIGHT: Bold;");

txtstream.OleFunction("WriteLine",OleVariant(\"  PADDING-BOTTOM: 3px;");

txtstream.OleFunction("WriteLine",OleVariant(\"  COLOR: white;");

txtstream.OleFunction("WriteLine",OleVariant(\"  PADDING-TOP: 3px;");

txtstream.OleFunction("WriteLine",OleVariant(\"  BORDER-BOTTOM: #999 1px
solid;");

txtstream.OleFunction("WriteLine",OleVariant(\"  BACKGROUND-COLOR: navy;");

txtstream.OleFunction("WriteLine",OleVariant(\"  FONT-FAMILY: font-family:
Cambria, serif;");

txtstream.OleFunction("WriteLine",OleVariant(\"  FONT-SIZE: 12px;");

txtstream.OleFunction("WriteLine",OleVariant(\"  text-align: left;");

txtstream.OleFunction("WriteLine",OleVariant(\"  display:table-cell;");
```

txtstream.OleFunction("WriteLine",OleVariant(\"   white-Space: nowrap;");

txtstream.OleFunction("WriteLine",OleVariant(\"   width: 100%;");

txtstream.OleFunction("WriteLine",OleVariant(\"}");

txtstream.OleFunction("WriteLine",OleVariant(\"h1 {");

txtstream.OleFunction("WriteLine",OleVariant(\"color: antiquewhite;");

txtstream.OleFunction("WriteLine",OleVariant(\"text-shadow: 1px 1px 1px black;");

txtstream.OleFunction("WriteLine",OleVariant(\"padding: 3px;");

txtstream.OleFunction("WriteLine",OleVariant(\"text-align: center;");

txtstream.OleFunction("WriteLine",OleVariant(\"box-shadow: inset 2px 2px 5px rgba(0,0,0,0.5);, inset -2px -2px 5px rgba(255,255,255,0.5);;");

txtstream.OleFunction("WriteLine",OleVariant(\"}");

txtstream.OleFunction("WriteLine",OleVariant(\"</style>\"))");

SHADOW BOX

txtstream.OleFunction("WriteLine",OleVariant(\"<style type='text/css'>\"))");

txtstream.OleFunction("WriteLine",OleVariant(\"body");

txtstream.OleFunction("WriteLine",OleVariant(\"{");

txtstream.OleFunction("WriteLine",OleVariant(\"   PADDING-RIGHT: 0px;");

txtstream.OleFunction("WriteLine",OleVariant(\"   PADDING-LEFT: 0px;");

txtstream.OleFunction("WriteLine",OleVariant(\"   PADDING-BOTTOM: 0px;");

txtstream.OleFunction("WriteLine",OleVariant(\"   MARGIN: 0px;");

txtstream.OleFunction("WriteLine",OleVariant(\"   COLOR: #333;");

txtstream.OleFunction("WriteLine",OleVariant(\"   PADDING-TOP: 0px;");

txtstream.OleFunction("WriteLine",OleVariant(\"   FONT-FAMILY: verdana, arial, helvetica, sans-serif;");

txtstream.OleFunction("WriteLine",OleVariant(\"}");

txtstream.OleFunction("WriteLine",OleVariant(\"table");

txtstream.OleFunction("WriteLine",OleVariant(\"{");

txtstream.OleFunction("WriteLine",OleVariant(\"   BORDER-RIGHT: #999999 1px solid;");

txtstream.OleFunction("WriteLine",OleVariant(\"   PADDING-RIGHT: 1px;");

txtstream.OleFunction("WriteLine",OleVariant(\"   PADDING-LEFT: 1px;");

txtstream.OleFunction("WriteLine",OleVariant(\"   PADDING-BOTTOM: 1px;");

txtstream.OleFunction("WriteLine",OleVariant(\"   LINE-HEIGHT: 8px;");

txtstream.OleFunction("WriteLine",OleVariant(\"   PADDING-TOP: 1px;");

txtstream.OleFunction("WriteLine",OleVariant(\"   BORDER-BOTTOM: #999 1px solid;");

txtstream.OleFunction("WriteLine",OleVariant(\"   BACKGROUND-COLOR: #eeeeee;");

txtstream.OleFunction("WriteLine",OleVariant(\" filter:progid:DXImageTransform.Microsoft.Shadow(color='silver', Direction=135, Strength=16");

txtstream.OleFunction("WriteLine",OleVariant(\"}");

txtstream.OleFunction("WriteLine",OleVariant(\"th");

txtstream.OleFunction("WriteLine",OleVariant(\"{");

txtstream.OleFunction("WriteLine",OleVariant(\"   BORDER-RIGHT: #999999 3px solid;");

txtstream.OleFunction("WriteLine",OleVariant(\"   PADDING-RIGHT: 6px;");

txtstream.OleFunction("WriteLine",OleVariant(\"   PADDING-LEFT: 6px;");

txtstream.OleFunction("WriteLine",OleVariant(\"   FONT-WEIGHT: Bold;");

txtstream.OleFunction("WriteLine",OleVariant(\"   FONT-SIZE: 14px;");

txtstream.OleFunction("WriteLine",OleVariant(\"   PADDING-BOTTOM: 6px;");

txtstream.OleFunction("WriteLine",OleVariant(\"   COLOR: darkred;");

txtstream.OleFunction("WriteLine",OleVariant(\"   LINE-HEIGHT: 14px;");

txtstream.OleFunction("WriteLine",OleVariant(\"   PADDING-TOP: 6px;");

txtstream.OleFunction("WriteLine",OleVariant(\" BORDER-BOTTOM: #999 1px solid;");

txtstream.OleFunction("WriteLine",OleVariant(\" BACKGROUND-COLOR: #eeeeee;");

txtstream.OleFunction("WriteLine",OleVariant(\" FONT-FAMILY: font-family: Cambria, serif;");

txtstream.OleFunction("WriteLine",OleVariant(\" FONT-SIZE: 12px;");

txtstream.OleFunction("WriteLine",OleVariant(\" text-align: left;");

txtstream.OleFunction("WriteLine",OleVariant(\" white-Space: nowrap;");

txtstream.OleFunction("WriteLine",OleVariant(\"}");

txtstream.OleFunction("WriteLine",OleVariant(\".th");

txtstream.OleFunction("WriteLine",OleVariant(\"{");

txtstream.OleFunction("WriteLine",OleVariant(\" BORDER-RIGHT: #999999 2px solid;");

txtstream.OleFunction("WriteLine",OleVariant(\" PADDING-RIGHT: 6px;");

txtstream.OleFunction("WriteLine",OleVariant(\" PADDING-LEFT: 6px;");

txtstream.OleFunction("WriteLine",OleVariant(\" FONT-WEIGHT: Bold;");

txtstream.OleFunction("WriteLine",OleVariant(\" PADDING-BOTTOM: 6px;");

txtstream.OleFunction("WriteLine",OleVariant(\" COLOR: black;");

txtstream.OleFunction("WriteLine",OleVariant(\" PADDING-TOP: 6px;");

txtstream.OleFunction("WriteLine",OleVariant(\" BORDER-BOTTOM: #999 2px solid;");

txtstream.OleFunction("WriteLine",OleVariant(\" BACKGROUND-COLOR: #eeeeee;");

txtstream.OleFunction("WriteLine",OleVariant(\" FONT-FAMILY: font-family: Cambria, serif;");

txtstream.OleFunction("WriteLine",OleVariant(\" FONT-SIZE: 10px;");

txtstream.OleFunction("WriteLine",OleVariant(\" text-align: right;");

txtstream.OleFunction("WriteLine",OleVariant(\" white-Space: nowrap;");

txtstream.OleFunction("WriteLine",OleVariant(\"}");

txtstream.OleFunction("WriteLine",OleVariant(\"td");

txtstream.OleFunction("WriteLine",OleVariant(\"{");

txtstream.OleFunction("WriteLine",OleVariant(\"   BORDER-RIGHT: #999999 3px solid;");

txtstream.OleFunction("WriteLine",OleVariant(\"   PADDING-RIGHT: 6px;");

txtstream.OleFunction("WriteLine",OleVariant(\"   PADDING-LEFT: 6px;");

txtstream.OleFunction("WriteLine",OleVariant(\"   FONT-WEIGHT: Normal;");

txtstream.OleFunction("WriteLine",OleVariant(\"   PADDING-BOTTOM: 6px;");

txtstream.OleFunction("WriteLine",OleVariant(\"   COLOR: navy;");

txtstream.OleFunction("WriteLine",OleVariant(\"   LINE-HEIGHT: 14px;");

txtstream.OleFunction("WriteLine",OleVariant(\"   PADDING-TOP: 6px;");

txtstream.OleFunction("WriteLine",OleVariant(\"   BORDER-BOTTOM: #999 1px solid;");

txtstream.OleFunction("WriteLine",OleVariant(\"   BACKGROUND-COLOR: #eeeeee;");

txtstream.OleFunction("WriteLine",OleVariant(\"   FONT-FAMILY: font-family: Cambria, serif;");

txtstream.OleFunction("WriteLine",OleVariant(\"   FONT-SIZE: 12px;");

txtstream.OleFunction("WriteLine",OleVariant(\"   text-align: left;");

txtstream.OleFunction("WriteLine",OleVariant(\"   white-Space: nowrap;");

txtstream.OleFunction("WriteLine",OleVariant(\"}");

txtstream.OleFunction("WriteLine",OleVariant(\"div");

txtstream.OleFunction("WriteLine",OleVariant(\"{");

txtstream.OleFunction("WriteLine",OleVariant(\"   BORDER-RIGHT: #999999 3px solid;");

txtstream.OleFunction("WriteLine",OleVariant(\"   PADDING-RIGHT: 6px;");

txtstream.OleFunction("WriteLine",OleVariant(\"   PADDING-LEFT: 6px;");

txtstream.OleFunction("WriteLine",OleVariant(\"   FONT-WEIGHT: Normal;");

txtstream.OleFunction("WriteLine",OleVariant(\"   PADDING-BOTTOM: 6px;");

txtstream.OleFunction("WriteLine",OleVariant(\" COLOR: white;");

txtstream.OleFunction("WriteLine",OleVariant(\" PADDING-TOP: 6px;");

txtstream.OleFunction("WriteLine",OleVariant(\" BORDER-BOTTOM: #999 1px solid;");

txtstream.OleFunction("WriteLine",OleVariant(\" BACKGROUND-COLOR: navy;");

txtstream.OleFunction("WriteLine",OleVariant(\" FONT-FAMILY: font-family: Cambria, serif;");

txtstream.OleFunction("WriteLine",OleVariant(\" FONT-SIZE: 10px;");

txtstream.OleFunction("WriteLine",OleVariant(\" text-align: left;");

txtstream.OleFunction("WriteLine",OleVariant(\" white-Space: nowrap;");

txtstream.OleFunction("WriteLine",OleVariant(\"}");

txtstream.OleFunction("WriteLine",OleVariant(\"span");

txtstream.OleFunction("WriteLine",OleVariant(\"{");

txtstream.OleFunction("WriteLine",OleVariant(\" BORDER-RIGHT: #999999 3px solid;");

txtstream.OleFunction("WriteLine",OleVariant(\" PADDING-RIGHT: 3px;");

txtstream.OleFunction("WriteLine",OleVariant(\" PADDING-LEFT: 3px;");

txtstream.OleFunction("WriteLine",OleVariant(\" FONT-WEIGHT: Normal;");

txtstream.OleFunction("WriteLine",OleVariant(\" PADDING-BOTTOM: 3px;");

txtstream.OleFunction("WriteLine",OleVariant(\" COLOR: white;");

txtstream.OleFunction("WriteLine",OleVariant(\" PADDING-TOP: 3px;");

txtstream.OleFunction("WriteLine",OleVariant(\" BORDER-BOTTOM: #999 1px solid;");

txtstream.OleFunction("WriteLine",OleVariant(\" BACKGROUND-COLOR: navy;");

txtstream.OleFunction("WriteLine",OleVariant(\" FONT-FAMILY: font-family: Cambria, serif;");

txtstream.OleFunction("WriteLine",OleVariant(\" FONT-SIZE: 10px;");

txtstream.OleFunction("WriteLine",OleVariant(\" text-align: left;");

txtstream.OleFunction("WriteLine",OleVariant(\" white-Space: nowrap;");

txtstream.OleFunction("WriteLine",OleVariant(\"   display: inline-block;");

txtstream.OleFunction("WriteLine",OleVariant(\"   width: 100%;");

txtstream.OleFunction("WriteLine",OleVariant(\"}");

txtstream.OleFunction("WriteLine",OleVariant(\"textarea");

txtstream.OleFunction("WriteLine",OleVariant(\"{");

txtstream.OleFunction("WriteLine",OleVariant(\"   BORDER-RIGHT: #999999 3px solid;");

txtstream.OleFunction("WriteLine",OleVariant(\"   PADDING-RIGHT: 3px;");

txtstream.OleFunction("WriteLine",OleVariant(\"   PADDING-LEFT: 3px;");

txtstream.OleFunction("WriteLine",OleVariant(\"   FONT-WEIGHT: Normal;");

txtstream.OleFunction("WriteLine",OleVariant(\"   PADDING-BOTTOM: 3px;");

txtstream.OleFunction("WriteLine",OleVariant(\"   COLOR: white;");

txtstream.OleFunction("WriteLine",OleVariant(\"   PADDING-TOP: 3px;");

txtstream.OleFunction("WriteLine",OleVariant(\"   BORDER-BOTTOM: #999 1px solid;");

txtstream.OleFunction("WriteLine",OleVariant(\"   BACKGROUND-COLOR: navy;");

txtstream.OleFunction("WriteLine",OleVariant(\"   FONT-FAMILY: font-family: Cambria, serif;");

txtstream.OleFunction("WriteLine",OleVariant(\"   FONT-SIZE: 10px;");

txtstream.OleFunction("WriteLine",OleVariant(\"   text-align: left;");

txtstream.OleFunction("WriteLine",OleVariant(\"   white-Space: nowrap;");

txtstream.OleFunction("WriteLine",OleVariant(\"   width: 100%;");

txtstream.OleFunction("WriteLine",OleVariant(\"}");

txtstream.OleFunction("WriteLine",OleVariant(\"select");

txtstream.OleFunction("WriteLine",OleVariant(\"{");

txtstream.OleFunction("WriteLine",OleVariant(\"   BORDER-RIGHT: #999999 3px solid;");

txtstream.OleFunction("WriteLine",OleVariant(\"   PADDING-RIGHT: 6px;");

```
txtstream.OleFunction("WriteLine",OleVariant(\"    PADDING-LEFT: 6px;");

txtstream.OleFunction("WriteLine",OleVariant(\"    FONT-WEIGHT: Normal;");

txtstream.OleFunction("WriteLine",OleVariant(\"    PADDING-BOTTOM: 6px;");

txtstream.OleFunction("WriteLine",OleVariant(\"    COLOR: white;");

txtstream.OleFunction("WriteLine",OleVariant(\"    PADDING-TOP: 6px;");

txtstream.OleFunction("WriteLine",OleVariant(\"    BORDER-BOTTOM: #999 1px
solid;");

txtstream.OleFunction("WriteLine",OleVariant(\"    BACKGROUND-COLOR: navy;");

txtstream.OleFunction("WriteLine",OleVariant(\"    FONT-FAMILY: font-family:
Cambria, serif;");

txtstream.OleFunction("WriteLine",OleVariant(\"    FONT-SIZE: 10px;");

txtstream.OleFunction("WriteLine",OleVariant(\"    text-align: left;");

txtstream.OleFunction("WriteLine",OleVariant(\"    white-Space: nowrap;");

txtstream.OleFunction("WriteLine",OleVariant(\"    width: 100%;");

txtstream.OleFunction("WriteLine",OleVariant(\"}");

txtstream.OleFunction("WriteLine",OleVariant(\"input");

txtstream.OleFunction("WriteLine",OleVariant(\"{");

txtstream.OleFunction("WriteLine",OleVariant(\"    BORDER-RIGHT: #999999 3px
solid;");

txtstream.OleFunction("WriteLine",OleVariant(\"    PADDING-RIGHT: 3px;");

txtstream.OleFunction("WriteLine",OleVariant(\"    PADDING-LEFT: 3px;");

txtstream.OleFunction("WriteLine",OleVariant(\"    FONT-WEIGHT: Bold;");

txtstream.OleFunction("WriteLine",OleVariant(\"    PADDING-BOTTOM: 3px;");

txtstream.OleFunction("WriteLine",OleVariant(\"    COLOR: white;");

txtstream.OleFunction("WriteLine",OleVariant(\"    PADDING-TOP: 3px;");

txtstream.OleFunction("WriteLine",OleVariant(\"    BORDER-BOTTOM: #999 1px
solid;");

txtstream.OleFunction("WriteLine",OleVariant(\"    BACKGROUND-COLOR: navy;");
```

```
txtstream.OleFunction("WriteLine",OleVariant(\"    FONT-FAMILY: font-family:
Cambria, serif;");

txtstream.OleFunction("WriteLine",OleVariant(\"    FONT-SIZE: 12px;");

txtstream.OleFunction("WriteLine",OleVariant(\"    text-align: left;");

txtstream.OleFunction("WriteLine",OleVariant(\"    display: table-cell;");

txtstream.OleFunction("WriteLine",OleVariant(\"    white-Space: nowrap;");

txtstream.OleFunction("WriteLine",OleVariant(\"    width: 100%;");

txtstream.OleFunction("WriteLine",OleVariant(\"}");

txtstream.OleFunction("WriteLine",OleVariant(\"h1 {");

txtstream.OleFunction("WriteLine",OleVariant(\"color: antiquewhite;");

txtstream.OleFunction("WriteLine",OleVariant(\"text-shadow: 1px 1px 1px black;");

txtstream.OleFunction("WriteLine",OleVariant(\"padding: 3px;");

txtstream.OleFunction("WriteLine",OleVariant(\"text-align: center;");

txtstream.OleFunction("WriteLine",OleVariant(\"box-shadow: inset 2px 2px 5px
rgba(0,0,0,0.5);, inset -2px -2px 5px rgba(255,255,255,0.5);;");

txtstream.OleFunction("WriteLine",OleVariant(\"}");

txtstream.OleFunction("WriteLine",OleVariant(\"</style>\"))");
```

www.ingramcontent.com/pod-product-compliance
Lightning Source LLC
Chambersburg PA
CBHW070845070326
40690CB00009B/1708